OPPOSING
VIEWPOINTS®
SERIES

# Organized Crime

# Other Books of Related Interest

**Opposing Viewpoints Series**

American Values

Community Policing

Criminal Justice

Hacking and Hackers

**At Issue Series**

Are Unions Still Relevant?

Child Pornography

Is Selling Body Parts Ethical?

Mexico's Drug War

**Current Controversies Series**

Espionage and Intelligence

Human Trafficking

Modern-Day Piracy

"Congress shall make
no law . . . abridging
the freedom of speech,
or of the press."

*First Amendment to the US Constitution*

The basic foundation of our democracy is the First Amendment guarantee of freedom of expression. The Opposing Viewpoints Series is dedicated to the concept of this basic freedom and the idea that it is more important to practice it than to enshrine it.

OPPOSING
VIEWPOINTS®
SERIES

# Organized Crime

*David Haugen, Susan Musser, and Michael Chaney,*
*Book Editors*

**GREENHAVEN PRESS**
*A part of Gale, Cengage Learning*

GALE
CENGAGE Learning·

Farmington Hills, Mich • San Francisco • New York • Waterville, Maine
Meriden, Conn • Mason, Ohio • Chicago

Elizabeth Des Chenes, *Director, Content Strategy*
Cynthia Sanner, *Publisher*
Douglas Dentino, *Manager, New Product*

*For more information, contact:*
Greenhaven Press
27500 Drake Rd.
Farmington Hills, MI 48331-3535
Or you can visit our Internet site at gale.cengage.com

Articles in Greenhaven Press anthologies are often edited for length to meet page requirements. In addition, original titles of these works are changed to clearly present the main thesis and to explicitly indicate the author's opinion. Every effort is made to ensure that Greenhaven Press accurately reflects the original intent of the authors. Every effort has been made to trace the owners of copyrighted material.

Cover image © sam100/Shutterstock.com.

**LIBRARY OF CONGRESS CATALOGING-IN-PUBLICATION DATA**

Organized crime / David Haugen, Susan Musser, and Michael Chaney, book editors.
      pages cm. -- (Opposing viewpoints)
  Includes bibliographical references and index.
  ISBN 978-0-7377-6965-4 (hardcover) -- ISBN 978-0-7377-6966-1 (pbk.)
  1. Organized crime. 2. Gangs. 3. Computer crimes. I. Haugen, David M., 1969- II. Musser, Susan. III. Chaney, Michael, 1949-
  HV6441.O7392 2014
  364.106--dc23

                                    2013049852

# Contents

## Chapter 3: What Policies Should Be Implemented to Address Organized Crime?

## Chapter 4: Has Organized Crime Moved Online?

# Why Consider Opposing Viewpoints?

> *"The only way in which a human being can make some approach to knowing the whole of a subject is by hearing what can be said about it by persons of every variety of opinion and studying all modes in which it can be looked at by every character of mind. No wise man ever acquired his wisdom in any mode but this."*
>
> John Stuart Mill

In our media-intensive culture it is not difficult to find differing opinions. Thousands of newspapers and magazines and dozens of radio and television talk shows resound with differing points of view. The difficulty lies in deciding which opinion to agree with and which "experts" seem the most credible. The more inundated we become with differing opinions and claims, the more essential it is to hone critical reading and thinking skills to evaluate these ideas. Opposing Viewpoints books address this problem directly by presenting stimulating debates that can be used to enhance and teach these skills. The varied opinions contained in each book examine many different aspects of a single issue. While examining these conveniently edited opposing views, readers can develop critical thinking skills such as the ability to compare and contrast authors' credibility, facts, argumentation styles, use of persuasive techniques, and other stylistic tools. In short, the Opposing Viewpoints Series is an ideal way to attain the higher-level thinking and reading skills so essential in a culture of diverse and contradictory opinions.

In addition to providing a tool for critical thinking, Opposing Viewpoints books challenge readers to question their own strongly held opinions and assumptions. Most people form their opinions on the basis of upbringing, peer pressure, and personal, cultural, or professional bias. By reading carefully balanced opposing views, readers must directly confront new ideas as well as the opinions of those with whom they disagree. This is not to simplistically argue that everyone who reads opposing views will—or should—change his or her opinion. Instead, the series enhances readers' understanding of their own views by encouraging confrontation with opposing ideas. Careful examination of others' views can lead to the readers' understanding of the logical inconsistencies in their own opinions, perspective on why they hold an opinion, and the consideration of the possibility that their opinion requires further evaluation.

## Evaluating Other Opinions

To ensure that this type of examination occurs, Opposing Viewpoints books present all types of opinions. Prominent spokespeople on different sides of each issue as well as well-known professionals from many disciplines challenge the reader. An additional goal of the series is to provide a forum for other, less known, or even unpopular viewpoints. The opinion of an ordinary person who has had to make the decision to cut off life support from a terminally ill relative, for example, may be just as valuable and provide just as much insight as a medical ethicist's professional opinion. The editors have two additional purposes in including these less known views. One, the editors encourage readers to respect others' opinions—even when not enhanced by professional credibility. It is only by reading or listening to and objectively evaluating others' ideas that one can determine whether they are worthy of consideration. Two, the inclusion of such viewpoints encourages the important critical thinking skill of objectively evaluating an author's credentials and bias. This evaluation will illuminate an author's reasons for taking a particular stance on an issue and will aid in readers' evaluation of the author's ideas.

It is our hope that these books will give readers a deeper understanding of the issues debated and an appreciation of the complexity of even seemingly simple issues when good and honest people disagree. This awareness is particularly important in a democratic society such as ours in which people enter into public debate to determine the common good. Those with whom one disagrees should not be regarded as enemies but rather as people whose views deserve careful examination and may shed light on one's own.

Thomas Jefferson once said that "difference of opinion leads to inquiry, and inquiry to truth." Jefferson, a broadly educated man, argued that "if a nation expects to be ignorant and free . . . it expects what never was and never will be." As individuals and as a nation, it is imperative that we consider the opinions of others and examine them with skill and discernment. The Opposing Viewpoints Series is intended to help readers achieve this goal.

*David L. Bender and Bruno Leone,*
*Founders*

# Introduction

> *"Criminal networks are not only expanding their operations, but they are also diversifying their activities, resulting in a convergence of transnational threats that has evolved to become more complex, volatile, and destabilizing."*
>
> —US President Barack Obama, *"Strategy to Combat Transnational Organized Crime,"* July 2011.

To most Americans, the term *organized crime* conjures up images of the Mafia—perhaps New York, Chicago, or Las Vegas mobsters with "family" connections stretching across the sea to Sicily, the home of the immigrants who first brought the "Cosa Nostra" ("Our Thing") to the United States in the late nineteenth century. But just as the term *Mafia* has been expanded in popular speech to include almost any unified crime network, the notion of organized crime has similarly broadened over time. As the title of the introductory Federal Bureau of Investigation webpage on organized crime trumpets, "It's not just the Mafia anymore." According to the FBI, those criminals who are now gathered under the label of organized crime in America include: "Russian mobsters who fled to the U.S. in the wake of the Soviet Union's collapse; groups from African countries like Nigeria that engage in drug trafficking and financial scams; Chinese tongs, Japanese Boryokudan, and other Asian crime rings; and enterprises based in Eastern European nations like Hungary and Romania." Broadening the definition, though, suggests that organized crime has taken on new meanings that coalesce around national identity and unity of criminal activity.

As the FBI webpages indicate, organized crime can be approached as an issue in which nationality plays a role. That is, the fall of the Soviet Union has led to the immigration of Russian gangsters and military personnel to the United States and other countries where they, in turn, form collectives that retain links to the major Soviet-era syndicates that spread their illicit claws into Russian and Central European industry, government, and prison systems. Likewise, African organized crime has utilized liberal government and trade structures in nations such as Liberia, Nigeria, and Ghana to expand local drug enterprises and fraud schemes across borders and continents. The FBI notes that ease of travel coupled with the globalization of information and economic networks have allowed these syndicates to crop up in the United States and in European nations. The FBI also contends that global connectedness is bringing these disparate groups together, "literally becoming partners in crime, realizing they have more to gain from cooperating than competing."

Perhaps it is the notion of cooperation that reflects the other way of classifying organized crime—by the type of crime perpetrated. While crime syndicates often deal in several nefarious activities simultaneously, pulling in profits from different illegal enterprises, it is common to attach significance to high-profile trade. For example, drugs have defined Mexican and Colombian cartels; intellectual property theft is tied to Chinese Triads. Other crimes, such as sports betting, human trafficking, money laundering, and illegal arms dealing have achieved public notoriety and are linked to criminal syndicates because they ostensibly have the networks and personnel to facilitate the efficient conduct of such activities. Smaller operations may even work in partnership with larger, organized gangs simply to take advantage of these networks. In a November 2004 resource paper on human trafficking written for Youth Advocate Program International, Robyn Skinner and Catherine Maher state that independents "benefit by affiliating with organized crime. For example, traffickers who are isolated in particular regions can expand their operations by collaborating with organized criminal groups that have connections in numerous locations around the world."

It is the reach of these larger organizations that is appealing. In fact, many law enforcement agencies subsume the concept of organized crime under the umbrella term *transnational crime* to reflect the power of syndicates that utilize information technologies and globalized trade realities to carry out their business on a worldwide scale. The United Nations Office on Drugs and Crime (UNODC) reiterates that "organized crime has diversified, gone global and reached macro-economic proportions: illicit goods may be sourced from one continent, trafficked across another, and marketed in a third." The UNODC remarks that because "organized crime transcends cultural, social, linguistic and geographical borders," law enforcement agencies must respond in kind, fighting criminal entities at an international level.

To wage collective action, the United Nations adopted the Convention Against Transnational Organized Crime (UNCTOC) in 2000, which went into effect in 2003. The instrument made countries aware of organized crime and pushed for cross-border assistance. As deputy assistant secretary of the Bureau of International Narcotics and Law Enforcement Affairs Elizabeth Verville remarked in a 2010 US State Department release, those nations that have ratified the convention are "committing themselves to its unique framework for cooperation, including mutual legal assistance, extradition, and uniform requirements for criminalizing serious crimes committed by organized crime groups." Verville noted that the United States had used the UNCTOC in twenty-five extradition cases from the convention's inception to its ratification. In 2011, the US National Security Council restated its pledge to fight transnational organized crime by not only working with other nations but also by "looking inward" to curb the illegal trade within America that fuels transnational organized crime. According to the National Security Council's "Strategy to Combat Transnational Organized Crime," this concerted effort would entail reducing the demand for drugs in the United States, going after weapons and finance merchants who deal with organized crime, and going after government and corporate corruption in the nation. Whether the renewed effort will find success is yet to be determined. As President Barack Obama cautions in his preamble to the strategy document, "Despite a long and successful history of dismantling criminal organizations and developing common international standards for cooperation against transnational organized crime, not all of our capabilities have kept pace with the expansion of 21st century transnational criminal threats." The president remains optimistic, though, in his remarks, insisting that the US strategy is in part a commitment to mutual action with global partners in confronting and curtailing transnational crime.

In *Opposing Viewpoints: Organized Crime*, the issues inherent in identifying and confronting organized crime are presented from several perspectives subsumed under four chapter titles that ask, Does Organized Crime Present a Threat to the World Today?, How Profitable Are Some Organized Crime Activities?, What Policies Should Be Implemented to Address Organized Crime?, and Has Organized Crime Moved Online? Expert authors debate the reach of organized crime, the degree of harm it causes, and the best methods for countering both. Some of these commentators examine the local impact of organized crime, while others focus on its transnational aspects. All share a concern for the expansion of such illicit activity and the manner in which it has kept pace with twenty-first-century technologies and economic practices. There is even a larger fear expressed by some of these authors that organized crime has conspired with corrupt governments, creating criminal states that take part in and reap rewards from illegal enterprises. Clearly, organized crime has outgrown its classic image in America. As this anthology emphasizes, modern governments, including Washington, DC, must continually reconceptualize the diversity, fluidity, and capabilities of organized crime if they are ever to successfully stymie its growth.

OPPOSING
VIEWPOINTS®
SERIES

# Does Organized Crime Present a Threat to the World Today?

# Chapter Preface

In November 2011, Viktor Bout, a Russian citizen, was convicted in a New York federal court for offering aid to terrorists and conspiring to kill Americans. Bout, then forty-four years old, was a former member of the Russian military and a businessman who had made his fortune running several air cargo transit companies. Some authorities believe he used his transport services to ship weapons and supplies to fuel civil wars in Africa during the 1990s. His fleet flew arms to Northern Alliance rebels in Afghanistan, and he reputedly brought gold and money out of the country on return trips. His questionable activities made him a wanted man by Interpol in 2002. In 2008, he was arrested in Thailand for agreeing to sell weapons to individuals he believed were representatives of the Revolutionary Armed Forces of Colombia (FARC), a rebel organization that both the United States and Colombia define as terrorist. In truth, the meeting had been set up by the Thai government and US Drug Enforcement Administration agents to trap Bout. He was extradited to the United States in 2010 under protest by the Russian government, which claimed in a Foreign Ministry statement that "long before the sentence against Bout was delivered, the government [had] anointed him the 'merchant of death' and practically an international terrorist." Though Bout professed his innocence, the US court found him guilty of the charges and sentenced him to twenty-five years in prison. It was a minimum sentencing because Bout did not successfully carry out his shipment, and no US citizens were consequently harmed. During the trial, Bout asserted that the charges were hypocritical, claiming that if the courts turned their attention to American arms dealers whose weapons sales eventually led to the death of US citizens, all legitimate merchants would be serving time.

Bout's career brought worldwide attention to organized arms smuggling. The 2005 movie *Lord of War* (starring Nicholas Cage as a Ukrainian American weapons merchant) borrows much from Bout's life and activities and presented the image of the callous opportunist ready to take advantage of murderous conflicts. In a March 2008 article for the *Guardian*, a British newspaper, Oliver Sprague, Amnesty International UK arms program director, claimed, "This is exactly why an international arms trade treaty is needed. Such a treaty would close loopholes that gun-runners like Viktor Bout so easily exploit for their own gain. Through their irresponsible arms transfers gun-runners like Bout have fuelled conflicts where dreadful human rights abuses have occurred." Indeed, in 2012, the United Nations drafted an arms trade treaty to regulate weapons trade and cut down on illegal practices. The document was signed by 113 countries in 2013 but has not yet been ratified by the required fifty member countries (including the United States).

Illegal arms trafficking is just one aspect of international organized crime. The World Economic Forum's Global Agenda Council on Organized Crime maintains that in an age of globalization, transnational communication networks, and free trade, criminal enterprises have made use of legitimate channels to further their nefarious ends and that therefore it is becoming more challenging to track illicit activity and disentangle it from aboveboard operations. On its website, the Global Agenda Council states, "Research has revealed intricate cooperation between the licit and illicit economies. Enablers of organized crime that are legitimate elements of the official economy include professional service providers, loosely monitored online data storage systems and complex supply chains." The connection between the two, the council asserts, has only recently earned greater attention by law enforcement. In the following chapter, several authorities speak out about local and global crime and debate whether it poses a threat to society and government in the twenty-first century.

"Organized crime has diversified, gone
global, and reached macro-economic
proportions[, which] is having an impact on security."

# Organized Crime Is a Threat to International Security

*Walter Kemp*

*Walter Kemp is director for Europe and Central Asia at the International Peace Institute and a former spokesman and speech writer for the United Nations Office on Drugs and Crime. In the following viewpoint, Kemp warns of the growing threat that organized crime presents to international security. He explains that organized crime is growing throughout the world due to globalization, weak governance, and corrupt governments. Kemp calls for a system-wide strategic response to make sure that organized crime prevention is part of the core of the United Nations' conflict-prevention program.*

As you read, consider the following questions:

1. Kemp notes that in the last twenty years, globalization has outpaced the growth of mechanisms for global governance, resulting in what?

Walter Kemp, "Organized Crime: A Growing Threat to Security," Stockholm International Peace Institute, February 10, 2010. Copyright © 2010 by SIPRI. All rights reserved. Reproduced by permission.

2. As stated by the author, what areas of the world are most vulnerable to organized crime?

3. According to Kemp, what has caused the phenomenon of the "criminalization of the state"?

On 24 February [2013] the UN Security Council will debate the issue of organized crime as a threat to international peace. The issue has also been hot in the G8 [the eight nations with the largest economies] and regional organizations like the OSCE [Organization for Security and Cooperation in Europe] and ECOWAS [Economic Community of West African States]. It is also getting a lot of attention in the media. Why is organized crime so high on the political agenda?

## A Lack of Regulation

In the last 20 years, globalization has outpaced the growth of mechanisms for global governance. This has resulted in a lack of regulation—whether it be on the Internet, in banking systems, or free trade zones. The same conditions that have led to unprecedented openness in trade, travel and communication have created massive opportunities for criminals. As a result, organized crime has diversified, gone global, and reached macro-economic proportions. This is having an impact on security.

Where control of the government is weak, criminals profit from instability. Such regions are sometimes called "ungoverned spaces", yet this is a misnomer because in many cases the sub-state entity is more effectively (if not democratically) administered than the internationally recognized state that it has broken away from. While the central government may not be willing or able to deliver public goods, collect taxes and provide public security, the de facto authorities manage to do all three—often on the basis of taxing or controlling illicit activity. Such an environment is advantageous to transnational criminal groups because it enables them to operate outside the law, but not in a complete state of anarchy (which is bad for business). It provides an efficient level of insecurity.

This creates a vicious circle: crime is attracted by insecurity, underdevelopment and weak governance, while the latter are exacerbated by crime.

Conflict or post-conflict areas are particularly vulnerable. In such areas, symbiotic [mutually beneficial] relationships can develop between anti-government forces and criminal groups. This is, or has been, evident in many danger zones, including Afghanistan, the Balkans, the Caucasus, Colombia, the Democratic Republic of the Congo [DRC], Peru, and parts of West Africa. Indeed, organized crime is present in almost every theatre where the UN carries out peacekeeping or peace-building operations.

In many cases, crime is a means to an end: it funds the anti-government struggle. But in some cases, criminal activity becomes so lucrative that political or ideological motivations become blurred with, or even trumped by, greed. Elements of the FARC [Revolutionary Armed Forces of Colombia] (cocaine), the [Cambodian] Khmer Rouge (ruby and teakwood), the Shining Path [Peruvian Communist Party] (cocaine), rebels in the DRC (gold) and the Taliban [fundamentalist Muslim party] (opium) have demonstrated this trait.

## Corrupting Governments from the Inside

In other cases, criminal groups operate more by stealth: seeking to coerce, corrupt or cajole state actors from the inside rather than teaming up with anti-government forces. In such cases, transnational criminal groups put pressure on senior officials in government, the judiciary, the police and the military in order to extract or traffic illicit goods, to operate with impunity and to buy power. They also use contacts in the private sector, for example for laundering money. This leads to the criminalization of the state, or at least many of its elite; for

# Crime and Migration

Migration poses multiple problems: it is often illegal and an increasingly lucrative activity for organized crime. First, the uprooting of people in their nations of origin puts additional strain on already fragile local societies. Second, the migratory flows tend to create temporary basins where people collect when they encounter obstacles on their road to opportunity: for example, Mali and Mauritania [in Africa] on the way to Spain and the Canary Islands; Morocco before the crossing of the Straits of Gibraltar; Tunisia and Libya before the attempt to cross over to Pantelleria and Lampedusa in Sicily, or mainland Italy; Egypt, into which an ever increasing number of migrants from Sudan and the Great Lakes area [of East Africa] migrate; Turkey, the springboard for the Balkan road into Europe; and Mexico, the gateway to the United States. . . .

Yet even if the migrants succeed and reach the *banlieus* [suburbs] of Paris or Marseille [in France], they often face insecurity, youth gangs, drugs, violence, and fundamentalist Islam. As recent terror attacks in Europe have shown, these young immigrants risk becoming the easy prey of radical preachers—thereby accelerating a vicious cycle of intercultural tension amid their own isolation.

*Theodor H. Winkler,*
*"The Shifting Face of Violence,"*
World Policy Journal, *Fall 2008.*

example, by building corrupt networks between business, crime, and politics. Under this arrangement, criminals effectively use all the trappings of the state to facilitate their activities: territorial waters, diplomatic passports, diplomatic pouches, immunity from prosecution, military facilities, intelligence information, even the state financial apparatus are exploited. They also influence the political process by funding political parties, or supporting key politicians. In return, their collaborators get rich. Some countries in West Africa and Central America are heading in this dangerous direction.

As a result, the state is hollowed out from the inside—captured by a crooked clique of self-serving cronies who hide their criminal activities behind a veil of legitimacy, use the proceeds of crime to build patronage networks and silence opposition by the threat or use of force (either the security services or the criminal groups). The social contract is replaced by a criminal bargain: criminal activity becomes state-sponsored, and in return the sponsors are protected and enriched by the criminals. The rule of law is replaced by the bullet and the bribe. This deepens corruption, compromises the integrity of state institutions and pushes common people into taking the law into their own hands. Collapse of the rule of law can also strengthen the appeal of political groups offering extreme alternatives, even authoritarian rule.

Whether profiting from "ungoverned spaces" or hollowing out the state from within, transnational criminal groups—plugged into global networks—gain control of key resources and/or trafficking routes that give them a profitable market share. The richer and more powerful they become, the greater the threat they pose to national, regional and global security as well as undermining development and the rule of law.

How can an international system, created to deal with tensions between states, confront non-state actors who become rich, powerful, and dangerous by respecting neither laws nor borders? This is a major challenge for the member states and the UN system as a whole.

Some solutions already exist, like the UN Convention against Transnational Organized Crime, which was adopted in Palermo [Italy] in December 2000. However, in the past decade the Convention has failed to live up to its potential. Parties to the Convention will meet later this year [2013] to see if they can strengthen its implementation.

For its part, the UN is looking for system-wide strategic response to organized crime by mainstreaming criminal justice into relevant activities, for example making sure that crime prevention and control are part of the core of the UN's conflict prevention, crisis management, and peacebuilding activities.

In the same way that there is a separate crime section in bookstores, organized crime used to be considered by policy makers as a dangerous yet isolated issue on the margins of international security. No longer. Crime has made its presence felt with a bang. As one of globalization's first movers, it has infiltrated deep into licit markets and high into government offices. The world is finally waking up to the threat.

| "Across the globe, criminals have pen-
etrated governments to an unprecedented degree."

# Governments Worldwide Have Been Corrupted by Organized Crime

*Moisés Naím*

*In the viewpoint that follows, Moisés Naím argues that in the current climate of economic crisis, organized crime syndicates and national governments have increasingly fused, creating international instability and potential upheaval. According to Naím, organized criminals have found that by providing funds to governments in need, they can gain positions of influence and exert power over the governments and, eventually, the countries as a whole. This is particularly dangerous, in the author's view, because it creates power players who do not obey the traditional rules of international policy and law, thus making their behaviors harder to predict and respond to. Naím maintains that national and international law enforcement must work together to address the security threats posed by these new mafia states. Naím is a senior associate in the International Economics Pro-*

Reprinted by permission of *Foreign Affairs*, vol. 91, no. 3, May–June 2012. Copyright © 2012 by the Council on Foreign Relations, Inc. www.ForeignAffairs.com.

*gram at the Carnegie Endowment for International Peace and a syndicated columnist and author who has written extensively about international policy issues.*

As you read, consider the following questions:

1. According to the study by Symantec that is cited by the author, how much did cybercrime cost the global economy in 2011?

2. In what ways have organized criminal gangs become involved in for-profit nuclear proliferation, as stated by Naím?

3. What are some of the new ways law enforcement officials worldwide have begun to fight organized crime as identified by the author?

The global economic crisis has been a boon for transnational criminals. Thanks to the weak economy, cash-rich criminal organizations can acquire financially distressed but potentially valuable companies at bargain prices. Fiscal austerity is forcing governments everywhere to cut the budgets of law enforcement agencies and court systems. Millions of people have been laid off and are thus more easily tempted to break the law. Large numbers of unemployed experts in finance, accounting, information technology, law, and logistics have boosted the supply of world-class talent available to criminal cartels. Meanwhile, philanthropists all over the world have curtailed their giving, creating funding shortfalls in the arts, education, health care, and other areas, which criminals are all too happy to fill in exchange for political access, social legitimacy, and popular support. International criminals could hardly ask for a more favorable business environment. Their activities are typically high margin and cash-based, which means they often enjoy a high degree of liquidity—not a bad position to be in during a global credit crunch.

## Organized Crime and Governments

But emboldened adversaries and dwindling resources are not the only problems confronting police departments, prosecutors, and judges. In recent years, a new threat has emerged: the mafia state. Across the globe, criminals have penetrated governments to an unprecedented degree. The reverse has also happened: rather than stamping out powerful gangs, some governments have instead taken over their illegal operations. In mafia states, government officials enrich themselves and their families and friends while exploiting the money, muscle, political influence, and global connections of criminal syndicates to cement and expand their own power. Indeed, top positions in some of the world's most profitable illicit enterprises are no longer filled only by professional criminals: they now include senior government officials, legislators, spy chiefs, heads of police departments, military officers, and, in some extreme cases, even heads of state or their family members.

This fusing of governments and criminal groups is distinct from the more limited ways in which the two have collaborated in the past. Governments and spy agencies, including those of democratic countries, have often enlisted criminals to smuggle weapons to allied insurgents in other countries or even to assassinate enemies abroad. (The CIA's [Central Intelligence Agency's] harebrained attempt to enlist American mafia figures to assassinate [Cuban leader] Fidel Castro in 1960 is perhaps the best-known example.) But unlike normal states, mafia states do not just occasionally rely on criminal groups to advance particular foreign policy goals. In a mafia state, high government officials actually become integral players in, if not the leaders of, criminal enterprises, and the defense and promotion of those enterprises' businesses become official priorities. In mafia states such as Bulgaria, Guinea-Bissau, Montenegro, Myanmar [formerly Burma], Ukraine, and Venezuela, the national interest and the interests of organized crime are now inextricably intertwined.

Because the policies and resource allocations of mafia states are determined as much by the influence of criminals as by the forces that typically shape state behavior, these states pose a serious challenge to policy makers and analysts of international politics. Mafia states defy easy categorization, blurring the conceptual line between states and non-state actors. As a result, their behavior is difficult to predict, making them particularly dangerous actors in the international environment.

## Faulty Assumptions

Conventional wisdom about international criminal networks rests on three faulty assumptions. First, many people believe that when it comes to illicit activities, everything has been done before. It is true that criminals, smugglers, and black markets have always existed. But the nature of international crime has changed a great deal in the past two decades, as criminal networks have expanded beyond their traditional markets and started taking advantage of political and economic transformations and exploiting new technologies. In the early 1990s, for example, criminal groups became early adopters of innovations in communications, such as advanced electronic encryption. Criminal syndicates also pioneered new means of drug transportation, such as "narco-submarines": semi-submersible vessels able to evade radar, sonar, and infrared systems. [Drug cartels in Colombia eventually graduated to fully submersible submarines.] In more recent years, criminal organizations have also taken advantage of the Internet, leading to a dizzying growth in cybercrime, which cost the global economy some $114 billion in 2011, according to the Internet security firm Symantec.

A second common misperception is that international crime is an underground phenomenon that involves only a small community of deviants operating at the margins of societies. The truth is that in many countries, criminals today do not bother staying underground at all, nor are they remotely marginal. In fact, the suspected leaders of many major criminal groups have become celebrities of a sort. Wealthy individuals with suspicious business backgrounds are sought-after philanthropists and have come to control radio and television stations and own influential newspapers. Moreover, criminals' accumulation of wealth and power depends not only on their own illicit activities but also on the actions of average members of society: for example, the millions of citizens involved in China's counterfeit consumer-goods industry and in Afghanistan's drug trade, the millions of Westerners who smoke marijuana regularly, the hundreds of thousands of migrants who every year hire criminals to smuggle them to Europe, and the well-to-do professionals in Manhattan and Milan who employ illegal immigrants as nannies and housekeepers. Ordinary people such as these are an integral part of the criminal ecosystem.

A third mistaken assumption is that international crime is strictly a matter of law enforcement best managed by police departments, prosecutors, and judges. In reality, international crime is better understood as a political problem with national security implications. The scale and scope of the most powerful criminal organizations now easily match those of the world's largest multinational corporations. And just as legitimate organizations seek political influence, so, too, do criminal ones. Of course, criminals have always sought to corrupt political systems to their own advantage. But illicit groups have never before managed to acquire the degree of political influence now enjoyed by criminals in a wide range of African, eastern European, and Latin American countries, not to mention China and Russia.

## The Emergence of Mafia States

In the past decade or so, this phenomenon has crossed a threshold, resulting in the emergence of potent mafia states.

# Perceived Government Corruption Worldwide, 2013

*Transparency International ranked 177 countries and territories around the world on their perceived levels of public sector corruption. Almost 70 percent of countries are perceived to have a serious corruption problem—a score lower than 50 out of 100. No country received a perfect score of 100.*

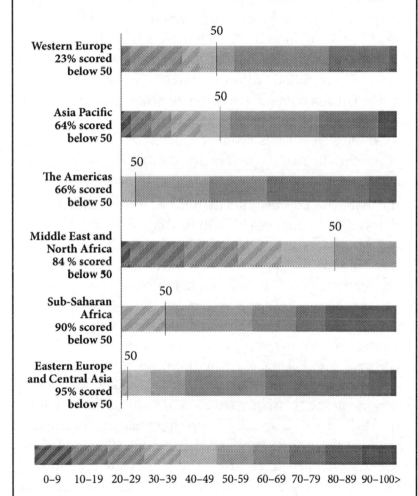

TAKEN FROM: Transparency International, "Infographics: Visualising the Corruption Perceptions Index 2013," http://cpi.transparency.org.

José Grinda, a Spanish prosecutor with years of experience fighting eastern European criminal organizations, maintains that in many cases, it has become impossible for him and his colleagues to distinguish the interests of criminal organizations from those of their host governments. According to Grinda, Spanish law enforcement officials constantly confront criminal syndicates that function as appendages of the governments of Belarus, Russia, and Ukraine. In confidential remarks contained in U.S. diplomatic cables released by the whistleblower Web site WikiLeaks, he detailed his concerns about the "tremendous control" exercised by what he termed "the Russian mafia" over a number of strategic sectors of the global economy, such as aluminum and natural gas. This control, Grinda suggested, is made possible by the extent to which the Kremlin [Russian government] collaborates with Russian criminal organizations.

In mafia states, government officials and criminals often work together through legal business conglomerates with close ties to top leaders and their families and friends. According to Grinda, Moscow regularly employs criminal syndicates—as when, for example, Russia's military intelligence agency directed a mafia group to supply arms to Kurdish rebels in Turkey. More indicative of the overlap between Russia's government and its criminal groups, however, is the case of a cargo ship, *Arctic Sea*, that the Russian government claimed was hijacked by pirates off the coast of Sweden in 2009. Moscow ostensibly sent the Russian navy to rescue the ship, but many experts believe it was actually smuggling weapons on behalf of Russia's intelligence services and that the hijacking and rescue were ruses intended to cover up the trafficking after rival intelligence services had disrupted it. Grinda says that the smuggling was a joint operation run by organized criminal gangs and what he cryptically termed "Eurasian security services." The Russians were embarrassed, but the outcome was essentially benign, even a bit comical. Still, the affair underscored the unpredictability of a security environment in which it is difficult to distinguish the geopolitical calculations of states from the profit motives of criminal organizations.

## Mafia Statehood Is Increasing

Russia is hardly the only country where the line between government agencies and criminal groups has been irreparably blurred. Last year [2011], the Council of Europe published a report alleging that the prime minister of Kosovo, Hashim Thaçi, and his political allies exert "violent control over the trade in heroin and other narcotics" and occupy important positions in "Kosovo's mafia-like structures of organized crime." The state-crime nexus is perhaps even stronger in Bulgaria. A 2005 U.S. diplomatic cable released by WikiLeaks last year is worth quoting at length, given the disturbing portrait it paints of Bulgaria's descent into mafia statehood. The cable read, in part:

> Organized crime has a corrupting influence on all Bulgarian institutions, including the government, parliament and judiciary. In an attempt to maintain their influence regardless of who is in power. OC [organized crime] figures donate to all the major political parties. As these figures have expanded into legitimate businesses, they have attempted—with some success—to buy their way into the corridors of power. . . . Below the level of the national government and the leadership of the major political parties. OC "owns" a number of municipalities and individual members of parliament. This direct participation in politics—as opposed to bribery—is a relatively new development for Bulgarian OC. Similarly in the regional center of Velingrad, OC figures control the municipal council and the mayor's office. Nearly identical scenarios have played out in half a dozen smaller towns and villages across Bulgaria.

This state of affairs led Atanas Atanasov, a member of the Bulgarian parliament and a former counterintelligence chief, to observe that "other countries have the mafia: in Bulgaria the mafia has the country." . . .

## Crime Creates Global Instability

In the past, foreign policy scholars generally considered international crime to be a relatively minor problem that domestic legal systems should handle. The impact of crime, they believed, was insignificant compared with the threat of terrorism or the proliferation of weapons of mass destruction. Fortunately, the conventional wisdom is starting to change. More and more experts and policy makers are recognizing that crime has become a significant source of global instability, especially with the emergence of mafia states.

Criminal gangs, for example, have become involved in for-profit nuclear proliferation. A.Q. Khan, the notorious Pakistani nuclear peddler, claimed that he was spreading bomb-making know-how to other nations in order to advance Pakistan's interests. But the international network he built to market and deliver his goods was organized as an illicit for-profit enterprise. Nuclear proliferation experts have long cautioned that non-state actors might not respond to nuclear deterrence strategies in the same way states do; there is reason to worry, then, that as criminal organizations fuse more thoroughly with governments, deterrence might become more difficult. Perhaps most worrisome in this regard is North Korea. Although North Korea recently announced that in exchange for food aid, it would suspend its nuclear weapons tests, stop enriching uranium, and allow international inspectors to visit its main nuclear complex, the country still remains a nuclear-armed dictatorship whose state-directed criminal enterprises have led U.S. officials to nickname it "the Sopranos state." Sheena Chestnut Greitens, an expert on the crime-state nexus in North Korea, has written that the country has "the means and motivation for exporting nuclear material," warning that "proliferation conducted through illicit networks will not always be well controlled by the supplier state," which adds additional uncertainty to an already dangerous situation.

Even putting aside the alarming prospect of nuclear mafia states, governments heavily involved in illicit trade might be more prone to use force when their access to profitable markets is threatened. Take, for example, the 2008 war between Georgia and Russia over the breakaway territories of Abkhazia and South Ossetia. According to the Carnegie Endowment's Thomas de Waal, an expert on the Caucasus, before the conflict, criminal organizations operated highly profitable operations in South Ossetia, where illicit trade accounted for a significant part of the economy. Although direct evidence is difficult to come by, the scale of these illegal activities suggested the active complicity of senior Russian officials, who acted as the criminals' patrons and partners. Of course, the conflict was fueled by many factors, including ethnic strife, domestic Georgian politics, and Russia's desire to assert its hegemony in its near abroad [i.e., neighbors]. But it is also conceivable that among the interest groups pushing the Kremlin toward war were those involved in lucrative trafficking operations in the contested areas.

Increasingly, fighting transnational crime must mean more than curbing the traffic of counterfeit goods, drugs, weapons, and people; it must also involve preventing and reversing the criminalization of governments. Illicit trade is intrinsically dangerous, but the threat it poses to society is amplified when criminals become high-level government officials and governments take over criminal syndicates. Yet today's law enforcement agencies are no match for criminal organizations that not only are wealthy, violent, and ruthless but also benefit from the full support of national governments and their diplomats, judges, spies, generals, cabinet ministers, and police chiefs. Mafia states can afford the best lawyers and accountants and have access to the most-advanced technology. Underfunded law enforcement agencies, overworked courts, and slow-moving bureaucracies are increasingly unable to keep up with such well-funded, agile foes. . . .

As the role of mafia states has become clearer, law enforcement officers across the globe have begun to develop new policies and strategies for dealing with such states, including requiring high-level public officials to disclose their finances; scrutinizing the accountants, lawyers, and technology experts who protect crime lords; and improving coordination among different domestic agencies. The rise of mafia states has also added urgency to the search for ways to internationalize the fight against crime. One promising approach would be to create "coalitions of the honest" among law enforcement agencies that are less likely to have been penetrated or captured by criminal groups. Some states are already experimenting with arrangements of this kind, which go beyond normal bilateral anticrime cooperation by including not just law enforcement agencies but also representatives from intelligence agencies and armed forces. A complementary step would be to develop multinational networks of magistrates, judges, police officials, intelligence analysts, and policy makers to encourage a greater degree of cooperation than Interpol affords by building on the trust that exists among senior law enforcement officers who have fought transnational criminal networks together for decades. As is often the case, long-term collaborations among like-minded individuals who know one another well and share values are far more effective than formal, officially sanctioned cooperation between institutions whose officers barely know one another.

Unfortunately, despite the near-universal recognition that combating international crime requires international action, most anticrime initiatives remain primarily domestic. And although mafia states have transformed international crime into a national security issue, the responsibility for combating it still rests almost exclusively with law enforcement agencies. Indeed, even in developed countries, police departments and other law enforcement bodies rarely coordinate with their national security counterparts, even though transnational crime threatens democratic governance, financial markets, and human rights.

An important obstacle to combating the spread of mafia states is a basic lack of awareness among ordinary citizens and policy makers about the extent of the phenomenon. Ignorance of the scope and scale of the problem will make it difficult to defend or increase the already meager budgets of government agencies charged with confronting international crime, especially in a time of fiscal austerity. But such awareness will be hard to generate while so many aspects of the process of state criminalization remain ill understood—and therein lies an even larger problem. Devoting public money to reducing the power of mafia states will be useless or even counterproductive unless the funds pay for policies grounded in a robust body of knowledge. Regrettably, the mafia state is a phenomenon about which there is little available data. The analytic frameworks that governments are currently applying to the problem are primitive, based on outdated understandings about organized crime. Addressing this dearth of knowledge will require law enforcement authorities, intelligence agencies, military organizations, media outlets, academics, and nongovernmental organizations to develop and share more reliable information. Doing so, however, would be only a first step—and an admittedly insufficient one.

*"The shooting of an innocent child . . . highlights the physical and emotional surcharges paid by families living in . . . gang-plagued neighborhoods."*

# Is It Safe to Walk to Church?

*Lawrence Harmon*

*In the following viewpoint, Lawrence Harmon tells the story of a thirteen-year-old boy that was shot and killed on his way to choir practice in Boston to highlight the ways in which communities suffer when subjected to control by criminal gangs. Harmon explains the descent into violence that some neighborhoods in Boston have experienced in recent years. In these situations, rival gangs have been waging war in the streets of certain neighborhoods making them unsafe even for community members and children who have no gang affiliation. Harmon is a columnist for the* Boston Globe.

As you read, consider the following questions:

1. Harmon cites the Reverend Eugene Rivers, who said that young teens in that area of Boston need what more than latitude?

2. According to the author, who is to blame for the rising violence in the area?

3. What reason is given by the author, for why the entire city of Boston owes a debt to the families that live in these gang-ridden areas?

"You live around here?" It sounds like an innocent question. But the exchange may have triggered the Jan. 11 shooting of a 13-year-old boy as he walked along Humboldt Avenue in Roxbury on his way to choir practice.

The victim, Gabriel Clarke, is about as far removed spiritually and mentally from Roxbury street life as possible. The middle schooler serves as a junior deacon at the Berea Seventh Day Adventist Church on Seaver Street in Dorchester. In the parlance of the church, Clarke has "Jesus on his mind." Now he is recovering from a stomach wound caused by a single shot from a blessedly small-caliber weapon.

One of the tenets of the Seventh Day Adventist faith is that God loves his people and wants to give them the highest quality of life imaginable. In Boston, however, quality of life is often determined by zip code.

## Gang-Plagued Neighborhoods

The shooting of an innocent child like Clarke highlights the physical and emotional surcharges paid by families living in the city's gang-plagued neighborhoods. For many Bostonians, urban life is defined by easy access to public transportation, nice restaurants, cultural venues, and houses of worship. But for others, like the Clarke family, living walking-distance to church can be a dangerous drawback.

Clarke's shooting was high on the agenda at last week's regularly scheduled Wednesday meeting at the Ella J. Baker House in Dorchester where officials from Boston Police and the MBTA [Massachusetts Bay Transportation Authority] trade intelligence with church leaders. Nearly to a minister, those around the table expressed surprise that the boy would be allowed to walk alone to choir practice at 7 o'clock on a Friday evening. The Rev. Jeffrey Brown, who will soon step down as head of the antiviolence TenPoint Coalition, and the Rev. Eugene Rivers, a Dorchester pastor, said that what young teens need more than latitude are rides to and from their extracurricular events in Roxbury and Dorchester.

"Most black professionals I know transport their kids from point A to point B," said Rivers. "Even when their kids are back from college." Brown takes the same approach with his 19-year-old daughter. "I'm there at the Shawmut T stop [in Dorchester] to take her home," he said.

Many Bostonians employ street safety skills such as walking in well-lighted areas and tucking packages securely between their arms and body. But a higher level of preparation is required to stay safe along Humboldt Avenue.

Boston Police reported rising tensions between the H Block gang, whose members live in the neighborhood where Clarke was shot, and other violent youth gangs in the city. Tensions are especially high between H Block and rival gangs from Heath Street in Jamaica Plain and Orchard Park in Roxbury. Staying current on such information can be the deciding factor in whether to allow a youngster to walk the few blocks between home and church. . . .

## Combating Gang Violence

Rivers said that the Berea Seventh Day Adventist Church in Dorchester operates outside this information loop. One reason, he said, is that many worshippers at the church drive in from local suburbs. Rivers and other ministers are hoping to convince pastors in and around Humboldt Avenue to replicate their weekly meetings with police. It makes sense. At such a meeting, ministers might have learned of the possibility of a retaliatory attack following an October shooting at the Bro-

## Gang Culture Results from Socioeconomic Factors

Because the image that most people have of the African-American community in South Central Los Angeles is one dominated by gangs, drugs, and violence, it becomes easy to assume that this must be the way it's always been, and thus that the spread of gang activity must somehow be connected with the very essence of African-American biology or culture itself. However, when placed in the context of the city's history, we see that African-Americans in Los Angeles managed to thrive and resist the descent into crime in spite of rampant racism, discrimination, and unemployment for more than a century and a half. The community stuck together, mutually solved the crises that plagued it and provided guidance and support for residents of all ages. Only when socioeconomic and social factors altered this unified community structure in such a way as to leave the youth abandoned and without guidance or direction did Los Angeles' inner-city African-American population began to make that fateful shift towards the gang and drug culture that is so pervasive today.

*Gregory Christopher Brown, James Diego Vigil,*
*and Eric Robert Taylor, "The Ghettoization*
*of Blacks in Los Angeles: The Emergence of Street Gangs,"*
*Journal of African American Studies, June 2012.*

mley Heath housing project or heard that young women associated with the rival gangs have been stirring up trouble on Facebook.

It's ungodly that so many families need to work this hard to stay safe. The entire city owes a debt to such families for remaining in place under such pressures. Without them, large swaths of Boston would resemble the bedraggled blocks of Baltimore, Philadelphia, and other US cities.

Meanwhile, there is something the [Mayor Thomas] Menino administration can do. It makes ample use of robo-calls to Boston homes for weather-related school cancellations and for public health purposes, such as flu shot reminders. It wouldn't hurt for people living in gang-infected neighbor-hoods to know when it isn't safe to walk to church.

▌ *"Gangs are good for society."*

# Gangs Create a Sense of Community for Youths

*Caspar Walsh*

*Caspar Walsh argues in the following viewpoint that gangs are not necessarily bad for society and can in some cases actually be good for young people. Walsh says that the media are largely responsible for creating the negative images of gangs and exaggerating the threat they pose to society. He maintains that gangs are good for young people because membership teaches them how to be part of a group with certain codes, which for many, is an important part of growing up. Walsh is an author and journalist and founder of the charity Write to Freedom.*

As you read, consider the following questions:

1. Walsh argues that much of the reported rise in youth crime is a result of what?

2. According to the author, why do young people join gangs?

3. Walsh says that in essence gangs are good for society because they do what?

"Gangs" get a bad press. The overused noun is now synonymous with the evils of youth culture and its incumbent violence, drugs, guns and sexual misconduct. There is a lot of rooftop shouting and table banging about the breakdown of teenage society: poor education, dysfunctional families, no respect for the older generations. "Wasn't like that when I was young." This dim view is, at best, misguided. At worst, clouded in denial and cushioned in the fiction of the nonexistent "good old days". Societies throughout history have each had their share of unlawful, out-of-control youth.

We hear a lot about an epidemic rise in youth crime. The truth is, youth crime has always been a part of society. It is how society deals with it that dictates its trajectory. Much of the reported rise in youth crime is in direct relation to the huge population increase in recent decades and, crucially, in the way the media choose to report youth crime.

## The Media Make Gangs Out to Be Bad

I put the blame for the de-meaning of the word gang squarely on the money hungry, narrative-driven media to ramp up our fear of the fiction of "gangs dominating every street corner". The issue is adrenalised in drama, documentaries and rolling news by repeatedly declaring "gang culture" as the cause of teenage societal meltdown. Gang culture is the widely accepted term used directly in connection with youth violence.

I've been working with young people both in and out of prison for more than 20 years, and what's clear is that gangs in and of themselves are not the problem. I was part of a gang in school and it was all about belonging to a group—it had nothing to do with fighting other gangs. It's when gangs start using violence to control turf and territory and make money that we need to take action. Young people join gangs because it is a crucial part of growing up. Gangs do not always revert to violence. If there are positive, older role models involved with these gangs, they can hold the boundaries es-

## Gangs as Surrogate Families

Understanding the underlying basis for gang membership is the key to answer the question as to why youth join gangs in the first place. One must also ask not just why they join but what motivates a youth to desire and acquire gang membership?

Those who have worked with these youths on the field and have gained their trust have heard the answer to this question. They join for a great number of reasons, including safety, friendship, status, recognition, curiosity, excitement, money, out of a sense of tradition due to generational commitment, peer pressure and drug abuse, just to name a few. Belonging to a gang gives them a sense of power and control over a specific geographic area, a certain group of people and even their own lives.

Feeling wanted and loved, giving and receiving love are essential expressions for a gang member, as for everyone in society. This is most evident in the way they commonly refer to the gang as their "family." Being part of a gang gives them a sense of belonging, of pride and honor. They feel they are accounted for and that they are contributing to something bigger than themselves. They also receive guidance, shelter and money. The gang becomes the member's sole source of survival, a surrogate or replacement family that provides positive reinforcement, direction, focus and a sense of purpose, which develops into a strong sense of blind commitment and loyalty.

*Henry R. Pacheco,*
*"Gangs 101: Understanding the Culture of Youth Violence,"*
*Esperanza, 2010. www.esperanza.us.*

sential to stopping them spiralling out of control and turning violent and crime driven. This is key.

Young people are looking for boundaries, and these are explored in gangs and in their social interactions with each other and people outside the gang circle. They will push the boundaries until they reach a wall they are either unable or unwilling to break down. This is an essential part of the process of growing up and becoming an active, law abiding member of society. The proliferation of violence in so many gangs in the UK is largely down to the absence of positive older role models holding the boundary line of acceptable behaviour. Without them, gang culture becomes toxic, loses its moral compass and often resorts to violence in dealing with power struggles and internal conflicts.

But there are many organisations working positively with young people in gangs and helping them through very difficult times in their lives, helping them through the often tough transition of evolving into productive, responsible members of society.

Having stopped my own death slide into crime, drugs and violence, I now choose to balance out media driven, moral "gang" panic with the many positive stories of reconciliation, rehabilitation and community reintegration that I hear about pretty much every day.

For me, gang is simply another word for tribe. In essence, gangs are good for society. In a healthy state, they are about the formation of groups that operate under ethical and moral codes of conduct upheld and enforced by the elders of the community. If these codes are based in a fundamental respect for society and the individual, there's absolutely nothing wrong with gangs. If the elders in the gangs have been supported and steered into responsible adulthood and are able in turn to guide and contain the fiery energy of future, younger gang members, society will be a far richer, more connected and ultimately less fearful place.

| "Organized crime is a human rights issue."

# Organized Crime Violates Human Rights

*Joy Olson*

*Human rights abuses perpetrated by organized crime groups have become the new battle that the human rights community must fight, according to Joy Olson in the following viewpoint. She argues that, while organized crime does not fit the traditional profile of human rights abusers, the human rights community must be flexible in its recognition of the changing landscape of human rights abuse and respond to any victims of abuse, no matter the perpetrator. To do this, Olson maintains, human rights defenders must reframe the current problem by placing the victims of violent organized criminals at the center of any debate on this issue and establish police and judicial institutions capable of fighting the criminals. Olson is the executive director of the Washington Office on Latin America and a human rights expert.*

As you read, consider the following questions:

1. As stated by the author, how many people have been killed in Mexico in connection with the drug war, drug trafficking, and organized crime since 2006?

2. Why is organized crime "worse than taking on the most dangerous dictator you can imagine" according to Olson?

3. What does Olson identify as the conviction rate for criminals in Mexico?

It was a horrifying scene—72 people murdered all at once. One survivor bore witness to the massacre. The dead were migrants, mostly Central Americans; 58 men and 14 women trying to make their way to a better future. It was August of 2010 when their bodies were found in Tamaulipas, Mexico. They were apparently killed by Mexico's most feared drug trafficking organization, the Zetas, who have diversified into other criminal activities like kidnapping and extortion.

This story made news for a few days. But the massacre shook me and made me start asking a lot of questions. Official reports said that the migrants were kidnapped off of buses. How could 72 people be kidnapped and no one notice? Bus drivers must have known something. The bus company must have noticed. Other travelers? Government authorities? How was this possible? Where is the outrage?

The human rights community and others, myself included, made statements about the massacre, but it did not become a central focus of coordinated human rights work. Most of us continued to work on our previously established agendas.

But why did it not have more impact?

Between 40,000 and 50,000 people have been killed in Mexico as a result of the drug war, drug trafficking, and organized criminal activities since 2006. About 3,000 people disappeared during Mexico's dirty war (late 1960s—early 1970s), a dark period in Mexican history. While other people have certainly disappeared since then, it is really the last time that "disappearance" was discussed as a phenomena or practice. Today the number is at least three times higher.

Again, where is the outrage? If numbers are any indicator, we should all be a lot more riled up.

Time progressed. Things haven't gotten better.

In April of 2011, mass graves were found in Tamaulipas, near where the earlier massacre took place. Close to 200 bodies were found. In May more mass graves were uncovered, this time in the state of Durango, containing nearly 300 bodies. Who were all of these people? Migrants? Criminals? People who got in the criminals' way?

Then there was the casino fire in Monterrey, Mexico, in which 52 people perished—not the result of faulty wiring, but of criminals tossing gas on a building and setting it ablaze. In September, 35 bodies were left along a city road in Veracruz, Mexico—near a shopping center—in broad daylight! Word got out fast because motorists started tweeting about masked men abandoning bodies.

These are just the really big cases.

Again, where is the human rights community, and what is our role? Or better yet, what should it be?

## Not Fitting the Human Rights Framework

I think I know at least in part why the violence in Mexico today has not been the focus of the human rights community. It is because this kind of violence doesn't fit the traditional human rights framework. Mexico is not unique in this respect. The murder rate in Central America was recently described in a UN report as nearing a "crisis point." Much of this violence is related to organized crime, as well as to gang activity. And while Mexico and Central America are in crisis mode, other countries in Latin America and beyond are suffering from violence associated with organized crime.

The work of human rights groups is based in international human rights law. That law, originating in the Universal Declaration of Human Rights, is focused on the responsibility of the state. It is states that sign and agree to abide by the treaties coming out of the Universal Declaration. Killings, torture, and disappearances carried out by the state are violations of human rights. On the other hand, killings, torture and disappearances carried out by the Zetas and other criminal organizations are crimes.

Yet there is a right to personal security. And even if the state is not directly violating that right, doesn't it have an obligation to protect its citizens? The Mexican state is not fulfilling that mandate, whether by commission or omission; it is not successfully arresting and prosecuting criminals. So where does the fundamental right of the citizen to security fit into the mandate of human rights organizations?

The fact that confronting organized crime is extremely dangerous work is another reason people have not jumped into this work. If you are a human rights defender on the ground, tackling organized crime is worse than taking on the most dangerous dictator you can imagine. People in the human rights community, again including me, don't know what they are up against with organized crime. We don't know the enemy. We don't know the rules of the game, so it's hard to know when you are going to get yourself or others into serious danger. We are not unique in this respect. Hardly anyone else does either.

## How to Combat Organized Crime

Then there is the question of how do you combat organized crime?

As human rights defenders we know how to influence the state. You hold people accountable. You demand transparency. You meet with officials and name the abuses. You use reason

## Mexican Officials Help Organized Crime

The majority of the likely enforced disappearance cases [in Mexico] follow a pattern. Members of security forces arbitrarily detain individuals without arrest orders or probable cause. In many cases, these detentions occur in victims' homes, in front of family members; in others, they take place at security checkpoints, at workplaces, or in public venues, such as bars. Soldiers and police who carry out these detentions almost always wear uniforms and drive official vehicles. When victims' relatives inquire about detainees' whereabouts at the headquarters of security forces and public prosecutors' offices, they are told that the detentions never took place. . . .

In cases where state agents work with organized crime in carrying out disappearances, the collaboration may take one of many different forms. Most commonly, security forces arbitrarily detain victims and then hand them over to criminal groups. Police, soldiers, and investigators may also work with criminal groups to extort the families of the victims, or tell those groups when victims' relatives report disappearances—information that abductors then use to harass and intimidate families. In more than a dozen cases, evidence pointed to state agents taking advantage of information obtained from families to pose as kidnappers and demand ransom from victims' relatives.

*Nik Steinberg,*
*"Mexico's Disappeared:*
*The Enduring Cost of a Crisis Ignored,"*
*Human Rights Watch, 2013.*

and appeal to common values and humanity. You protest. You name and shame abusers. You take people to court You seek to change laws.

Few of the strategies we have used in the past seem directly relevant to today's challenge of confronting organized crime. So, how do you tackle violations of human rights and human dignity when the violence is perpetrated not by the state but by non-state actors like organized crime?

Yet an anti-organized crime and a pro-human rights agenda do have something in common: respect for the rule of law. This in turn requires functioning, rights-respecting justice and police systems. If these institutions work properly, criminals are arrested and prosecuted, and state officials committing human rights violations are similarly held accountable.

But, for whatever reason, the human rights community has not fully embraced an anti-violence/organized crime or institutional reform agenda.

The Mexican state is failing miserably at protecting its citizens and holding criminals accountable. The conviction rate for crime in Mexico is two—yes I said two—percent. And there is rampant corruption and complicity of the state in organized crime. When institutions of justice fail so completely, it should be of central concern to people dedicated to human rights.

Now, there are exceptions to what I'm about to say and this does not apply only to Mexico, but for whatever reason, the human rights community has been stuck in an agenda that was developed in another era when the state was the principal perpetrator of abuse, when non-state actors were armed combatants in wars, and where the international law of war applied. Most human rights organizations in Latin America were founded during that era.

The traditional agenda of human rights organizations still reflects that era. It is an agenda that in Mexico includes ending military court jurisdiction over cases of military abuses against civilians (which has been absurdly difficult). And as for prosecuting emblematic cases of state abuse, often cases there are over a decade old (again because of the justice system taking an absurdly long time).

## Victims of Organized Crime

While these are important issues, violence related to organized crime is the proverbial elephant in the room.

In Mexico this conceptual division between organized crime and human rights violations is one reason that people have not come together to confront the violence, and certainly not under the human rights framework.

This is starting to change.

Earlier this year [2012], the son of Mexican poet Javier Sicilia was murdered by those involved in organized crime. Sicilia went public with his pain and called on the nation to stop the violence. He helped organize the Movement for Peace and Justice, marches across Mexico and silent protests against the violence. This movement has given voice to the victims and forced the president to dialogue with them. They have put the victims—not the criminals—at the center of the debate. Indeed, they are advocating for human rights.

Does the violence facing Mexico originating in organized crime technically fit the legal definition of human rights? Is it a human rights issue because there is corruption and state complicity with organized crime? Or is it a violation of human rights because of the state's failure to protect the victims?

Does that really matter?

Whether your son or daughter is killed by a drug trafficker or a corrupt police official, your pain is the same. Either way, you want and deserve justice. Confronting traditional human rights violations and criminal activity both require the same thing—functioning police and judicial institutions.

The human rights community is a vital resource for change. Today, the challenges to human rights are coming from different forces than those in the past. If our community doesn't change its agenda to address issues related to organized crime, an enormous opportunity for impact will be missed. If we do not act, victims will continue suffering in obscurity, the state will be threatened by criminals, and the concept of human rights will no longer be relevant.

Organized crime is a human rights issue and needs to be taken up by the human rights community—my community.

"*Mafias and cartels today pose the biggest threat to media freedom worldwide.*"

# Organized Crime Threatens Open Media Reporting

*Reporters Without Borders*

*In the following viewpoint, Reporters Without Borders, an international organization dedicated to defending freedom of information worldwide, describes the problems that reporters around the world face today as a result of organized crime, arguing that because reporters cannot report accurately on the topic, the problem cannot be adequately addressed. The authors contend that threats of violence against reporters have led them to censor themselves and not report on organized crime. When they do report on the issue, the author argues, they often use official police or government sources that do not accurately portray the problem. Further, the reports on arrests that are made grab headlines, but do little to actually decrease the incidence of organized crime, according to the authors. Reporters Without Borders maintains that this is a global problem affecting media in all countries that must be addressed to combat organized crime.*

As you read, consider the following questions:

1. According to the journalist from Ciudad Juárez quoted by Reporters Without Borders, what dangers do journalists in that city face?

2. As stated by the author, what happened to the Serbian radio station B92 after it questioned the financing of Delta Holding?

3. What are the disadvantages of tying organized crime arrests to the Italian mafia, according to Professor Bagley, as cited by the author?

A total of 141 journalists and media workers were killed during the decade of the 2000s in attacks and reprisals blamed on criminal groups. Mafias and cartels today pose the biggest threat to media freedom worldwide. A transnational phenomenon, organized crime is more than the occasional bloody shoot-out or colourful crime story in the local paper. It is a powerful parallel economy with enormous influence over the legal economy, one the media have a great deal of difficulty in covering. Its elusiveness and inaccessibility to the media make it an even greater threat, both to the safety of journalists and to the fourth estate's [aka, the press] investigative ability.

"Organized crime" is the generic label that the post–Cold War world has given to these new predators of journalism. Mafias, cartels, warlords recycled as traffickers, paramilitaries running rackets, separatist groups that traffic and extort to fund themselves—they have replaced the world's remaining dictatorial regimes as the biggest source of physical danger to journalists.

From newspapers to TV news, from crime reports to yellow press, the media seem to be reduced to counting the number of dead, including the dead within their own ranks. While organized crime often overlaps with a violent criminality consisting of rackets, kidnapping and murder, it is the expression of an economic and geopolitical reality that the media usually do not reflect, a reality that does not admit analysis of the types of criminal organizations involved, the way they operate and their ramifications.

This dimension of organized crime, which is completely beyond the scope of the 24-hour news cycle, also includes its impact on the "legal world" and its various components, including the media. Far from wanting to overthrow the political, economic and media bases of societies, organized crime has every interest in participating in them and using them. This fundamental fact suggests that the media are vulnerable not just as victims but also as actors or cogs of a parallel system for which they can serve as information and public relations outlets. . . .

## Threats Lead to Self-Censorship

The media can barely survive when they are directly targeted by criminal organizations. The emblematic example is Mexico, which has been enduring a federal offensive by 50,000 soldiers against the drug cartels since December 2006, as well as bloody turf wars among the cartels themselves. Around 35,000 people have been killed in this undeclared war, including more than 15,000 in 2010 alone. The Pacific cartel, Gulf cartel, Michoacán's Familia, Sinaloa cartel and Los Zetas are the leading players in this criminal hot-house which could not have prospered without a generalized decay in the Mexican state, the complicity of many officials and the lack of an adequate international response to the trafficking problem.

"The mere fact of being known to be journalists puts us in danger," we were told by a journalist in Ciudad Juárez, one of the epicentres of the federal offensive. "Either we are tortured and killed or we live under a permanent threat, not so much because of what we report, since there is so much self-censorship, but because of what we know or what we are assumed to know."

Shootings, decapitations, sometimes a military counterattack, less often a significant seizure—such is the daily fare of the media in the provinces—when they are not being directly attacked themselves. Obliged to chase after the news and constantly exposed to danger, most journalists do not succeed in providing anything more than quick and superficial coverage that is often third-rate.

"In these conditions, it is impossible to do an analysis or in-depth treatment of crime and drug-trafficking," said Claudia Méndez of *El Periódico*, one of the leading dailies in Guatemala, where the "Mexican effect" now compounds the more traditional violence inherited from the civil wars. "All the media do is just react to shootouts," she added. . . .

## The Media as Tools of Organized Crime

Who do you talk to? How do you verify? What sources can you use? In such a chaotic and impenetrable situation, the media often become a tool for spreading one crime organization's bad publicity about a rival organization—publicity for which they can pay dearly in the form of reprisals. The Sinaloa cartel "is blamed" [for] this execution. Los Zetas "are suspected" of being responsible for that massacre. Criminal organizations are also concerned about their reputations and have long understood that media represent a strategic interest. Under threat and with limited resources, the media often end up restricting themselves to just quoting official sources—a paradox given the public's limited confidence in the authorities in conflict zones.

Abandoning by-lined investigative reporting or indeed any kind of articles about crime and just using police communiqués is an option taken by many local media in Mexico but even this offers no safety guarantees. The cartels regard the authorities as competitors and even their bad publicity can cost dearly. The self-censorship adopted by *El Mañana*, a daily based in Nuevo Laredo, in the northeastern state of Tamaulipas, failed to prevent an attack with heavy weapons on its premises in February 2006.

When the authorities are the only source, coverage is liable to [be] compromised. "Their collusion with organized crime is well known, although hard to evaluate," a journalist in the Balkans said on condition of anonymity. "Politicians have a clear interest in controlling the news and much less interest in protecting journalists. More or less direct censorship and pressure, especially financial pressure, are other obstacles to real investigative reporting and encourage self-censorship." He cited the case of the Serbian radio station *B92*, which quickly found it had very little advertising after it raised questions about the financing of Delta Holding, a manufacturing, retail and services conglomerate that represents about 40 per cent of Serbia's economy.

The situation is just as stark in Iraqi Kurdistan, where the first anniversary of the kidnapping and murder of independent journalist Sardasht Osman [was] celebrated on 4 May [2011]. "Either the media depend financially on the authorities, and they ask no questions, or the media are really independent, in which case they get no response from the authorities," a local journalist told us. "In Kurdistan, the right to receive and impart news and information is not accompanied by any legal guarantees. This discourages journalists from questioning the authorities." . . .

## Obscuring a Complex Reality

A quarter of the cocaine produced in Colombia transits through Venezuela, where there were 18,000 murders in 2010, according to unofficial sources. Javier Mayorca, head of crime reporting at the Caracas-based *El Nacional* daily, says official sources are of limited use. "Information about everyday and large-scale crime is controlled very tightly by the Venezuelan government and its agencies," he said. "This is all the more so since President Hugo Chávez broke off all cooperation with the US Drug Enforcement Administration in 2005. We are forced to use outside sources. The authorities are concerned about the country's image. They don't want to appear powerless. So their information is biased."

Such an attitude is only to be expected from overwhelmed governments, which are more able to announce spending plans than to claim lasting successes. Under the Merida initiative, the United States spent 1.6 billion dollars on trying to combat drug trafficking in Mexico, Central America, Haiti and the Dominican Republic from 2007 to 2010. Under Plan Colombia, launched 10 years earlier, more than 7 billion dollars were spent on a similar goal, mainly for controversial military operations. But with what result? Ninety percent of the 85,000 firearms seized in the past four years of the war on drug trafficking in Mexico came from the United States. The rejection by the US Congress in 2004 of an Assault Weapon Ban restricting the sale of high-calibre firearms has had a major impact in Mexico, and on the results of the military offensive. Highly-publicized announcements and statistics, combined with ad hoc media coverage, all help to obscure the complex reality.

## The Media Are Impotent

"Do arrests of Mafiosi serve any purpose?" asked a provocative headline by *Slate.fr* journalists Margherita Nasi and Grégoire Fleurot last December [2010]. The photo accompanying the article showed Antonio Iovine, identified as the head of the Neapolitan Camorra [i.e., the mafia in Naples, Italy], with a triumphant expression, surrounded by embarrassed-looking policemen and carabinieri [national police force]. The story did not say whether Domenico Giorgi, a member of the Cala-

## Police and Media Perceptions of Most Important Organized Crimes to Cover

*Order of importance: Most important = 1; Least important = 15.*

| Criminal activities | Police Managers | Media |
|---|---|---|
| Hard drugs production and trafficking | 3.11 | 3.67 |
| Drug import and export | 3.44 | 4.06 |
| Intimidation of justice officials | 4.50 | 5.65 |
| Money laundering | 4.94 | 8.81 |
| Intimidation/extortion of the public | 5.28 | 5.35 |
| Soft drugs production and trafficking | 6.06 | 7.31 |
| Economic crimes (telemarketing scams, securities fraud, etc.) | 6.50 | 8.33 |
| Weapons trafficking | 7.44 | 8.24 |
| Smuggling | 7.89 | 9.35 |
| Prostitution procurement | 8.76 | 9.88 |
| Migrant smuggling | 9.11 | 7.83 |
| Environmental crimes (illegal disposal of hazardous waste, etc.) | 9.17 | 10.29 |
| Auto theft (networks) | 9.59 | 10.38 |
| Counterfeiting | 10.05 | 12.06 |
| Gambling | 12.22 | 12.63 |

TAKEN FROM: Judith Dubois, "Media Coverage of Organized Crime—Police Managers Survey," *Trends in Organized Crime*, vol. 7, no. 4, Summer 2002.

brian 'Ndrangheta [an Italian mafia] who was arrested two days later in Turin, managed to give his arrest the same appearance of a publicity coup.

Accused Jamaican druglord Christopher "Dudus" Coke, also known as "The President," managed to maintain his reputation as a philanthropist in the West Kingston neighbourhood of Tivoli Gardens until his arrest in May 2010 after a month-long siege, and then to portray himself as the injured party when his government extradited him to the United States. The most spectacular aspect of the raids on US branches of Cosa Nostra [Sicilian mafia] in the states of New York, New Jersey and Rhode Island on 20 January was the number of people arrested—127—of whom 91 were suspected of belonging to the five leading Italian-American crime families (Genovese, Gambino, Lucchese, Colombo and Bonanno). The story had all the right keywords—raid, godfather and mafia—and the pictures to go with it. A godsend for the media but not necessarily for the fight against organized crime.

"Such images have the disadvantage of identifying organized crime with the traditional figure of Don Vito Corleone," University of Miami's Professor [Bruce] Bagley [a specialist in organized crime] said, alluding to Marlon Brando's famous role in *The Godfather*. "It also suggests that organized crime has the relatively centralized, pyramid structure that characterizes traditional Italian mafias. But not all organized crime follows this model."

Even in Italy, La Magliana—a gang made famous by the film *Romanzo Criminals*, which sometimes did jobs for the mafia and sometimes did "counter-terrorist" work for the state during the political extremism of the 1970s—operated mainly as a network of partners and associates that was very different from the family structure of the 'Ndrangheta or, originally, Cosa Nostra. "A raid or an arrest is a ready-made media story and focuses on faces, but it has no effect on the general dynamic of organized crime," Bagley said.

The French criminologist Xavier Raufer made the same point when he referred ironically in an interview for *Slate.fr* to "the trick of making the media think that a particular crime organization is the most important one or that a particular mafioso is the most wanted crime boss." It makes little difference that Domenico Giorgi is behind bars when, according to the *Mafia.fr* research website, an estimated 155 'Ndrine

('Ndrangheta families) with 7,000 members are responsible for 3 per cent of Italy's GNP [gross national product].

## Romanticizing Crime Leaders

Colombian journalist Maria Teresa Ronderos, the founder of the Verdad Abierta website, cautions against any tendency to romanticize crime figures or the organizations they head. "The Colombian press has too often portrayed paramilitary chiefs such as Salvatore Mancuso or traffickers such as Pablo Escobar as colourful and invincible individuals, great business minds and sometimes protectors. The traumatized Colombian public logically remembers that the paramilitaries were responsible for more than 1,000 major massacres and 45,000 disappearances in a decade. But these paramilitary regional groups, like the cartels, have also become the tools of a much bigger economic—and sometimes political—system in which everything is quickly replaceable and interchangeable." And often behind the scenes.

How are the trafficking routes organized and controlled? How are organized crime networks established and maintained? What financial channels and arrangements are used to cross the frontiers between the parallel economy and the legal economy? Covering organized crime from the limited perspective of everyday crime stories clearly fails to address these questions. And the challenge concerns the industrialized countries as well as the developing ones, democratic states as well as authoritarian regimes. No media anywhere can claim to be better equipped than others for the challenge.

# Periodical and Internet Sources Bibliography

*The following articles have been selected to supplement the diverse views presented in this chapter.*

| | |
|---|---|
| Jay S. Albanese | "Deciphering the Linkages Between Organized Crime and Transnational Crime," *Journal of International Affairs*, Fall/Winter 2012. |
| Peter Andreas | "Gangster's Paradise," *Foreign Affairs*, March/April 2013. |
| Tom Barker | "American Based Biker Gangs: International Organized Crime," *American Journal of Criminal Justice*, September 2011. |
| Bruce Lawlor | "The Black Sea: Center of the Nuclear Black Market," *Bulletin of the Atomic Scientists*, November 2011. |
| Michael Levi | "States, Frauds, and the Threat of Transnational Organized Crime," *Journal of International Affairs*, Fall/Winter 2012. |
| Arthur J. Lurigio and John J. Binder | "The Chicago Outfit: Challenging the Myths About Organized Crime," *Journal of Contemporary Criminal Justice*, May 2013. |
| Gary Moore | "Mexico's Massacre Era," *World Affairs*, September/October 2012. |
| Sarah Percy and Anja Shortland | "The Business of Piracy in Somalia," *Journal of Strategic Studies*, August 2013. |
| Christina M. Ruetschlin and Abdul Karim Bangura | "Transnational Organized Crime: A Global Concern," *Journal of International Diversity*, 2012. |

# CHAPTER 2

# How Profitable Are Some Organized Crime Activities?

# Chapter Preface

In 2012, the United Nations Office on Drugs and Crime (UNODC) released figures that estimated the annual profits of worldwide organized criminal activity at $870 billion. Counterfeiting accounted for roughly $250 billion of that total, but far larger were the earnings of drug trafficking. According to the UNODC, the sale of drugs rakes in $320 billion a year, the largest percentage of organized crime's illicit profits. That amount surpasses the net economic revenues of countries like Russia and Switzerland, and it is nearly twice as much as the income of the oil-rich nation of Saudi Arabia.

The illegal drug market specializes in the cultivation, distribution, and direct sale of its products across the globe. The trade is divided up by organized gangs and cartels that manage logistics and keep supply chains in operation. In nations such as Mexico, the cartels operate like both industries and armies, paying off officials and purchasing small arms to protect their territories. In a July 26, 2013, report, Agence France-Presse, an international newswire, quotes UNODC head Yuri Fedotov as stating, "Gangs are better funded than any law enforcement institution." The implication is that law enforcement agencies lack the manpower and, in some cases, firepower to keep these criminal networks in check.

According to the 2012 US Senate Caucus on International Narcotics Control, the United States continues to be the largest consumer market for illicit drugs. Using statistics from a 2010 National Survey on Drug Use and Health, the Senate Caucus estimated that 22.6 million Americans aged twelve and up are current drug users. Also in 2012, the White House released findings that approximated consumer spending on the top four illegal drugs (marijuana, cocaine, methamphetamine, and heroin) at $100 billion. These figures may correlate to an overall rise in illicit drug use in America (from 8.7 percent of the population in 2009 to 8.9 percent in 2010), as noted by the National Survey on Drug Use and Health.

The illegal drug industry is so profitable, experts say, because the cost of manufacturing is so low while the export value is so high. The US street value of Colombian cocaine, for example, is between ten to twenty times its value at home. A former Drug Enforcement Administration agent told the PBS news program *Frontline* in the late 1990s that "the average drug trafficking organization, meaning from Medellín [the main drug-trafficking city in Colombia] to the streets of New York, could afford to lose 90% of its profit and still be profitable." Several US officials and foreign leaders argue that the way to reduce these profits is for governments—especially the US government—to consider legalizing parts of the drug trade. In a December 2009 article for the *Wall Street Journal*, David Luhnow reported that three former Latin American presidents—Ernesto Zedillo of Mexico, Cesar Gaviria of Colombia and Fernando Henrique Cardoso of Brazil—spoke in favor of legalization of marijuana as a way to curtail the violence associated with the illegal drug cartels. Luhnow's review quotes sources who believe the war on drugs is being improperly executed because Washington mistakenly approaches drug trafficking as a law-and-order issue instead of a business enterprise that understands markets and supply networks. Noting this vocal opposition to current policy, Luhnow writes, "Advocates for drug legalization say making marijuana legal would cut the economic clout of Mexican cartels by half [because] marijuana accounts for anywhere between 50% to 65% of Mexican cartel revenues." Those who support America's tough stance on drugs counter with the potential social harms of widespread drug legalization. In a March 2012 tour through Mexico, US vice president Joe Biden affirmed that drug legalization would cause bureaucratic headaches and public health crises.

In the chapter that follows, commentators give their opinions on the profitability of sectors of organized crime. Some suggest the revenues have been overstated, while others offer reasons why these "businesses" are so lucrative and detrimental to both legitimate economies and consumer populations.

> "As a form of transnational organized crime, ... the production and sale of counterfeit goods is a global, multi-billion dollar problem."

# Counterfeit Goods Are Profitable for Organized Crime

## UN Office on Drugs and Crime

*The counterfeiting of goods including food, medicine, and retail products, among others, by organized crime syndicates generates billions of dollars for criminals, according to the UN Office on Drugs and Crime (UNODC). The UNODC argues in the following viewpoint that this organized crime activity puts the lives of people around the world at risk because when people buy counterfeit goods, they are getting a product that is often of much lower quality than expected. This difference in quality could produce a product that is at worst fatal, but even when not deadly, can be ineffective. The UNODC works at an international level to stop this counterfeiting by organized crime and encourages people to take action locally to combat this crime by not purchasing goods that may be counterfeit. The UNODC is the United Nations office tasked with assisting member states in the fight against illegal drugs and international organized crime.*

United Nations Office on Drugs and Crime, "Trafficking in Persons," *The Globalization of Crime: A Transnational Organized Crime Threat Assessment*, UNODC, 2010.

As you read, consider the following questions:

1. What are five examples of counterfeit goods produced by organized crime identified by the author?

2. What percentage of fraudulent pharmaceuticals make up the drug market in Asia, Africa, and Latin America, according to the author?

3. As stated by the UNODC, how many containers of counterfeit goods has the Container Control Programme seized?

Counterfeiting is estimated by the Organisation for Economic Co-operation and Development (OECD) to generate some $250 billion a year in criminal proceeds. As a form of transnational organized crime, counterfeiting forms part of a new campaign by the UN Office on Drugs and Crime (UNODC)....

The production and sale of counterfeit goods is a global, multi-billion dollar problem and one that has serious economic and health ramifications for Governments, businesses and consumers. Counterfeiting is everywhere—it can affect what we eat, what we watch, what medicines we take and what we wear—and all too often the link between fake goods and transnational organized crime is overlooked or underestimated.

## A Serious Health Concern

Counterfeiting is a wide ranging crime which typically includes the practice of manufacturing goods, often of inferior quality, and selling them under a brand name without the owner's authorization. Counterfeiters are involved in the illegal production of knock-offs in virtually every area—food, drinks, clothes, shoes, pharmaceuticals, electronics, auto parts, toys, currency, tickets for transport systems and concerts, alcohol, cigarettes, toiletries, building materials and much, much more. Criminals rely on the continued high demand for cheap goods coupled with low production and distribution costs.

Depending on the nature of the counterfeit goods, there can be serious health and safety concerns for consumers. Counterfeit baby formula and other foods can even be fatal, while purchases such as substandard toys, car parts and electrical goods present significant safety risks given their lower quality.

One of the most harmful forms of counterfeit goods is fraudulent medicines. According to the World Health Organization, in parts of Asia, Africa and Latin America, fraudulent pharmaceuticals amount to as much as 30 per cent of the market. These types of medicines are found either to contain the wrong dose of active ingredients, or none at all, or to have a completely different ingredient included. These medicines make some of the world's most dangerous diseases such as malaria stronger by contributing to the development of drug-resistant strains, as the active ingredients are no longer able to work correctly.

## A Local and an International Fight

With the counterfeit business spread across numerous countries and organized by criminal networks, there is an ever-growing need for action at both the local and international levels. The United Nations Convention against Transnational Organized Crime, of which UNODC is the guardian, is the world's most inclusive platform for cooperation in tackling all forms of organised crime. Currently, 167 countries are party to the Convention and have committed themselves to fighting organized crime through collaboration and ensuring that domestic laws are suitably structured. . . .

Through its technical assistance programmes, UNODC also works to counter the flow of illicit goods such as counterfeit products and drugs. UNODC and the World Customs Organization launched the Container Control Programme (CCP)

## Organized Crime and Illicit Antiquities

There is no clear distinction between the licit and the illicit antiquities markets. Archaeological materials are traded on the same market, regardless of whether they have been tainted by an illegal act. Ricardo J. Elia of Boston University has explained, "People think that there is an illicit and a legitimate market. In fact, it is the same." It is worth noting that not all participants in the illegal trade are illegal actors; legal actors often participate in illegal transactions, either knowingly or unknowingly.

This makes identifying distinct criminal groups in the context of the illicit antiquities trade difficult. Motivation for illegal acts ranges from profit, to ideology, to neuroses. Some groups are organized for the purpose of engaging in the illegal trade, while others participate only incidentally. Organizations range in size from transnational criminal syndicates to family-run operations.

Despite the oft-repeated assertion that organized crime controls the illicit trade, there has been little scholarly treatment of the claim.

*Kimberly L. Alderman,*
*"Honor Amongst Thieves:*
*Organized Crime and the Illicit Antiquities Trade,"*
Indiana Law Review, *2012.*

in 2006. The programme has achieved remarkable results, seizing 487 containers of fraudulent and contraband goods alongside a further 195 containers of drugs. This year alone [2012], the programme has led to the seizure of 19 containers with over 100 tons of fake Tramadol, a pain-killer, all originating in India and seized in West Africa. The CCP presently has

28 operational port control units across 14 countries and is receiving increased interest from the private sector as the counterfeit seizures grow.

But fighting counterfeiting is not just the role of international organizations, public health authorities, trade organizations or consumer groups. Concerned citizens have a role to play too. In this, UNODC advocates for the following actions: If you know a film has been illegally copied and is being sold as a knock-off, do not buy it. If your favourite designer brand is clearly not made by your favourite designer, stay away. Beyond these obvious counterfeit products, stay alert to other warning signs. If a medicine that you know normally requires a prescription is available online without any sort of script from a doctor, then it could harm your health, perhaps irreversibly. Remember—while these purchases may save you money in the short term, the longer-term losses are far more costly.

> *"That there is a massive problem of or-*
> *ganized criminal DVD and CD street*
> *piracy in the US . . . has little to do*
> *with present day piracy."*

# Organized Crime's Involvement in Media Piracy Is Exaggerated

*Joe Karaganis*

*In the viewpoint that follows, Joe Karaganis, writer, editor, and vice president of the American Assembly at Columbia University, contends that the reports on the threat of media piracy and its ties to organized crime are greatly exaggerated. These hyped claims often come from within the entertainment industry, according to the author, as evidenced by the example of the portrayal of the problem on the show* Crime Inc. *In Karaganis's view, this program misrepresented all the information it presented about media piracy to coincide with the entertainment industry's desire to overstate the problem so laws to stop piracy will be enacted. Karaganis maintains that this approach spreads misinformation about the complicated problem of piracy and its causes.*

As you read, consider the following questions:

1. What does Karaganis believe the story of piracy to be about?

2. According to the Copy Culture survey cited by the author, what percentage of Americans have ever purchased a pirated DVD?

3. What advance does the author believe will end Mexican crime cartel involvement in the street sale of pirated DVDs?

Growing up in Chicago in the 1970s and 1980s, I have fond memories of watching Bill Kurtis on Channel 2 news. He was sort of a local Walter Cronkite [iconic American broadcast journalist and CBS news anchor]—the personification of the news. At our house, he was on every night.

So I felt some nostalgia when I got a call from a staffer on Kurtis' current show, *Crime Inc.*, about an episode they wanted to do on media piracy. And also some apprehension, since we've been pretty adamant in our work that criminality—and especially organized crime—is the wrong way to look at piracy. But since I'm a regular complainer about press coverage of these issues and an optimist that the debate can be changed, I agreed to help.

The *Crime Inc.* people sent over an outline that leaned heavily on content industry talking points: job losses attributable to piracy; financial losses to Hollywood, artists, and the economy; downloading as theft; and the role of organized crime.

But they had also found our *Media Piracy in Emerging Economies* report and wanted to understand our perspective. I explained that we have problems with the way the major industry groups frame these issues. We don't think piracy is primarily a crime story, but rather about prices, lack of availability, the changing cultural role of media, and the irreversible spread of very cheap copying technologies. They said they understood. It's a complicated topic.

I said I'd help as long as this didn't end up as an MPAA [Motion Picture Association of America] propaganda piece. [TV newsmagazine] *60 Minutes* had done one of those a couple years ago and it was a major public disservice. They said they'd do their best.

## Bowing to Industry Pressure

Over the next few months I spent four or five hours talking to and corresponding with staff at *Crime Inc.* I walked them through the difficulties with measuring the impact of piracy, the problems with opaque industry research, the general irrelevance of organized crime, the market structure and price issues that have made piracy an inevitability in the developing world, the wider forms of disruption in the music industry and so on, and so on. I gave them a list of people to talk to, including Internet hero and MPEE [Media Piracy in Emerging Economies] support group gold member Mike Masnick. And they did interview Mike for several hours.

The episode aired a few weeks ago. Unfortunately, it is an almost pure propaganda piece for the film and music industry groups, reproducing the tunnel vision, debunked stats, and scare stories that have framed US IP [intellectual property] policies for years. Nothing I told them registered. Mike did not appear. The only concession was two minutes at the end for an alternative business model segment focused, strangely, on the Humble Bundle software package [bundles of digital games for which users pay what they want].

By the end, I no longer thought this was an MPAA covert op. Rather it looked like a Rick Cotton overt op. Cotton is VP [vice president] and General Counsel at NBC-Universal, an enforcement hardliner and piracy fabulist to rival Jack Valenti [former president of the MPAA], and one of *Crime Inc.*'s corporate bosses at NBC-Universal. He got plenty of airtime to talk about the existential crisis of piracy and the need for stronger enforcement. I have no idea if word came down from him to produce this story (it was the early days of the SOPA [Stop Online Piracy Act] fight) or if *Crime Inc.* was just following the well-worn script on these issues. One doesn't exclude the other. But it is clear that the show rented itself out to Cotton's larger enterprise: *Crime Inc.* Inc., the business of hyping the piracy threat.

## Many Piracy Claims Are Myths

So what do we learn from *Crime Inc.* Inc.? Here's a short summary. I'll also reproduce some of my end of my correspondence with them below, which goes into more detail.

First—and bizarrely—that there is a massive problem of organized criminal DVD and CD street piracy in the US. And that this is part of a much wider array of linked criminal activities; and that DVD piracy is more lucrative than the drug trade.

I imagine they led with this because it's more filmable, but it has little to do with present day piracy. I tried to tell them that. Our work does go into this and finds what everyone knows—that DVD piracy has been displaced by sharing and downloading of digital files in the US in the past decade, and that the street trade has been almost completely marginalized. Even at its peak, CD/DVD piracy does not appear to have been a big market. Our 2011 "Copy Culture" survey found that only 7% of American adults had ever bought a pirated DVD. The drug trade claim—-ugh. It's incredible that this bit of nonsense can be endorsed by journalists with some investment in understanding crime.

Second—we get a recitation of impossible-to-kill zombie stats: that media piracy costs the global economy $57 billion/year; that it costs the movie business $6.2 billion/year; that 2 million people work in film/TV production in the US and

## Early Book Piracy

From the early days of the book trade in the fifteenth century, cultural markets were shaped by deals within the publishing trade and with political authorities over who could reproduce works and on what terms. While printers and publishers sought protection from competition, state and church authorities wanted to control the circulation of texts. Regulations designed to serve these goals led to a highly centralized printing trade in most European countries, in which state-favored publishers monopolized local markets.

Such monopolies inevitably attracted competitors from the ranks of the less privileged printers, as well as from those outside local markets. Repeatedly, over the next centuries, state-protected book cartels were challenged by entrepreneurs who disregarded state censorship, crown printing privileges, and guild-enforced copyrights. Already in the early seventeenth century, incumbent publishers labeled such printers pirates, evoking maritime theft and plunder.

Such conflicts were not limited to local markets. Pirate printers tended to flourish at the geographical peripheries of markets—often across borders, where the enforcement power of the state stopped. Scottish and Irish publishers competed with London publishers for English audiences; Dutch and Swiss publishers printed for the French market under the ancien régime [prerevolutionary France]. To a considerable extent, the European sphere of letters emerged through this transnational explosion of print.

*Bodó Balázs, in* Media Piracy in Emerging Economies, *ed. Joe Karaganis, 2011.*

that piracy has destroyed 373,000 jobs. The problems with these numbers will be familiar to readers of this site. . . .

Third—the now traditional guided tour of Mexican street markets, to look for evidence of cartel manufacture of CDs and DVDs. . . . This has become a media ritual. In short: are cartels involved? Almost certainly yes, in parts of Mexico where the cartels control most of the informal (and some of the formal) economy. Is this typical of developing countries or the US? No. Will it survive the spread of bandwidth and cheap computers in Mexico? No.

Fourth—that downloading is theft and everyone knows it. End of story. Pity the hipster they found to stage this point. We document more complicated attitudes toward copying and sharing in the US, marked by generally strong concern with the ethics of uploading or "making available" of materials; widespread but weak and largely non-operative concerns with downloading; and virtually no concerns about sharing with friends and family.

Fifth—that piracy is why sympathetic characters like a Hollywood stuntwoman have to worry about not having steady jobs or insurance. This is an odd claim in an era of record profits for the major studios, massive corporate welfare for film production, and continued outsourcing of production to non-union, low-wage countries, but hey—it's a show about piracy.

Sixth—that the SOPA debate was about—I kid you not— "Hollywood vs. high-tech thievery." Censorship or innovation concerns? No. (Skip to the very end for this somewhat garbled line. I imagine some embarrassed producer telling host Carl Quintanilla to just mumble through it and get it over with.)

## The Most Powerful Anti-Piracy Strategy

That's not a full list, but life is short and *Crime Inc.* has already absorbed too much of mine. I'll add that watching this on Hulu in several sittings was a maddening experience in itself since Hulu resets with every viewing, force feeding the same 90 second Buick LaCrosse commercial each time. (How has this viewer annoyance system survived? And how is this targeted advertising for someone living in Manhattan?)

Uncharacteristically, there appear to be no pirated versions of the episode available online. Which leads me to think that *Crime Inc.* may have stumbled onto the most powerful anti-piracy strategy of all: make TV that's only designed to please the corporate boss.

| *"Organized crime has . . . developed a greater resemblance to the activities of law-abiding businesses."*

# Organized Crime Has Come to Resemble Legitimate Business

*Marc Goodman*

*As the business world has incorporated technological and efficiency innovations into their business models, so too has organized crime. This is the argument Marc Goodman makes in the following viewpoint, and he furthers this by contending that legitimate business could benefit from the implementation of other tactics utilized by organized crime groups. Goodman points out five areas in which organized crime groups have adopted businesslike approaches to advance their criminal activity, including taking advantage of opportunities to make money on the basis of news stories; bringing in specialists to do specific jobs; emphasizing incentives beyond just monetary rewards; engaging in multiple, smaller criminal actions instead of one big one to maximize profits; and teaming up with other organized crime groups when it furthers both groups' goals. The author urges business managers to be aware of the tactics used by organized crime, not only to know the enemy, but also to utilize the ideas that work within a legal business. Goodman is an adviser to law enforcement agencies and the founder of the Future Crimes Institute.*

As you read, consider the following questions:

1. What scam did organized crime enact following the earthquake in Haiti, according to Goodman?

2. How does the author say that most organized crime groups make money off of credit card fraud?

3. What does Goodman identify as one of the benefits of cross-border organized crime partnerships?

When 10 men attacked the Taj Mahal Palace hotel in Mumbai, in November 2008, they executed one of the best-orchestrated, most technologically advanced terrorist strikes in history. Before the assault they had used Google Earth to explore 3-D models of the target and determine optimal entry and exit routes, defensive positions, and security posts. During the melee they used BlackBerrys, satellite phones, and GSM [Global System for Mobile Communications] handsets to coordinate with their Pakistan-based command center, which monitored broadcast news and the Internet to provide real-time information and tactical direction. When a bystander tweeted a photo of commandos rappelling from a helicopter onto the roof of one of the buildings, the center alerted the attackers, who set up an ambush in a stairwell. It took three days for authorities to kill nine of the terrorists and arrest the tenth; his confession provided details of the operation, which had resulted in 163 deaths and hundreds of injuries.

Atrocities like this one are an extreme example, but the fact remains that technology is increasingly put to nefarious uses. Consumers and businesses must deal with the results, from small-bore, almost laughable "I'm stranded in England please send money" e-mail scams to large-scale appropriations of credit card data. During the 25 years I've spent in law enforcement—as a police officer, a counterterrorism consultant, and, for the past decade, a cyber-risk and intelligence specialist—the most striking trend I've seen is the growing sophistication of global crime syndicates and terrorists (the former are now believed to bring in $2 trillion a year). Some of this isn't new: Colombian drug cartels, for instance, have been technologically advanced since the days of [late-eighties TV crime drama] *Miami Vice*. But more-recent international crime groups, including the Russian Business Network, South America's Superzonda, and the worldwide ShadowCrew, have become especially adept at expropriating legitimate business tactics to create highly efficient global teams and set new best practices in adaptive strategy, supply chain management, the use of incentives, global collaboration, and other disciplines. Here are five lessons companies can learn from the activities of such groups.

## Exploiting Newsworthy Events

Criminal groups have made an art of scanning the environment and quickly deploying technology to capitalize on what they find. Within hours of the 2010 Haiti earthquake, for example, scammers were circulating e-mails urging people to use Western Union to wire money to the British Red Cross. The cause sounded noble—but the British Red Cross doesn't accept donations by way of Western Union. Ever-adaptive criminals are also creating "Text this number to donate $10" scams after disasters.

Thieves are exploiting long-term technology trends as well. While corporations struggled to monetize their social media followers, criminals quickly figured out that tweets and Facebook updates were invaluable tools for planning home burglaries and that social media data could facilitate identity

© Grisela/www.CartoonStock.com

theft. *The lesson: Watch the headlines, move quickly, and try to get out in front of developing trends.*

## Recruiting Specialists

Outsource to specialists. Modern organized crime has abandoned the top-heavy structure of dons, capos, and lieutenants made famous in *The Godfather*. Most of today's gangs, along with Al Qaeda and other terrorist groups, are loosely affiliated cooperative networks—and are as likely to recruit website designers and hackers as they are thugs and enforcers. They routinely turn to niche markets for specific expertise. (For instance, Dubai offers the best talent for laundering money.) They are constantly networking to develop sources with the specialized skills they need, much as Hollywood studios scout for talent to cast a given film. For example, identity theft specialists know where to find artists who can replicate the holograms on ID and credit cards, and they routinely utilize a call center in Russia whose multilingual employees work 24/7 and are accomplished at making fraudulent calls to banks during which they might impersonate anyone from a rich Italian housewife to a Brazilian doctor. *The lesson: Don't limit yourself by overreliance on in-house talent. Cultivate e-lancers and other contractors who can provide the precise skills your project demands.*

## Finding Meaning in the Job

Cash isn't the only incentive. Criminal organizations pay well, both to compensate for the legal risks involved and because their high profit margins allow them to. But they realize that team members usually aren't in it just for the money. Most enjoy the thrill of breaking the law. Many, particularly hackers, are also motivated by the challenges of sophisticated security systems and the bragging rights they gain when they foil them. Although criminal organizations still employ a fair share of thugs, they're increasingly attracting highly educated people who seek autonomy and intellectual stimulation—not unlike the people who are drawn to the risky, demanding work environment of a start-up. *The lesson: Socially oriented businesses aren't the only ones that can use workers' desire for meaning as a motivating force. Find a way to tap into employees' needs for recognition, challenge, and belonging.*

## Many Smaller Jobs Increase Profits

Exploit the long tail. Until the Internet came along, many criminals pursued a "blockbuster" approach: They were always on the lookout for a single heist—say, a bank robbery—that could provide a huge payoff. Terrorists still strive for spectacular attacks, seeking to maximize the societal shock and disruption. But global criminals have learned that they can reap big profits by executing smaller operations over and over again—a strategy that allows for efficiency gains, continual improvement, and reduced risk. If you've ever been the victim of credit card fraud, you probably noticed a flurry of midsize purchases, usually made online; these can be received and forwarded by a "mule" who may not even realize he's part of an illegal scheme. (Syndicates often tell such mules they're part of an import-export operation.) The purchases on any one card might not exceed $1,000. Multiply that amount by thousands of transactions, though, and the payoff becomes huge. The perpetrators of small but high-volume frauds also constantly conduct experiments aimed at improving results. They may use different subject lines in the same e-mail scam, comparing the response rates and then fine-tuning the language in the next round. *The lesson: A business model that aims for many small transactions instead of a single big hit can result in larger long-term profits and provide numerous opportunities to improve efficiency along the way.*

## Partnering with Others

Collaborate across borders. Various radical Islamic splinter groups now work alongside Al Qaeda, even though the entities remain distinct. So, too, with organized crime: The Hong Kong–based triads and the Japanese Yakuza have joined forces to market synthetic drugs, and Colombia's cartels cooperate with Russian and Eastern European mafias to expand the reach of their products. Although "going global" has been an important way for businesses to extend market opportunities, the strategy delivers an additional benefit to organized crime: It can create legal obstacles for law enforcement officials, who often aren't as adept at cross-border collaboration as the criminals they're tracking. *The lesson: Don't look at competitors simply as rivals. Consider the mutual benefits of partnerships.*

## Organized Crime Is Innovative

Comparing the practices of criminal and terrorist organizations with those of corporations is by definition an imperfect exercise. Despite their sophistication and managerial prowess, crime groups are unconcerned with the human and social costs of their acts; they will remain ruthless no matter how many computer scientists they employ. But it's also true that as organized crime has come to rely more on technology for competitive advantage, its craft has developed a greater resemblance to the activities of law-abiding businesses. In some cases, criminal enterprises are now the ones pushing the frontiers of knowledge and innovation. Given the high profitability of global cybercrime networks and the limited threat they face from legal authorities, legitimate businesses will undoubtedly become targets more frequently. Managers need to pay close attention to the tactics being used against them—and perhaps even learn to profit from some of the global gangsters' insights.

*"The main difference between the banks and the Mafia is that [banks] effectively have licenses to act the way they do."*

# Wall Street Has Come to Resemble Organized Crime

*Paul Wallis*

*In the viewpoint that follows, Paul Wallis argues that Wall Street bankers, stockbrokers, and other financial companies have become much like organized crime in their lawless actions and corrupt behavior. He first highlights the billions of dollars collected by Wall Street entities through fraudulent investment practices by citing the extensive* Rolling Stone *article on the topic by Mark Taibbi. He goes on to make a more direct comparison between Wall Street and the Mafia as depicted in Roberto Saviano's book* Gomorrah, *focusing on disregard for people's lives. Much of this, Wallis contends, can be blamed also on politicians and their duplicitous behavior that allows these firms to do whatever they want as long as they pay off the right people in government. Wallis concludes with a lament of the plaguelike state of white-collar crime and blames the government of colluding with criminals. Wallis is a digital journalist working out of Sydney, Australia, who contributes regularly to the* Digital Journal.

As you read, consider the following questions:

1. According to the *Rolling Stone* article cited by Wallis, what are some examples of the amounts of money that banks have made fraudulently?

2. What are some of the examples given by the author that exhibit Wall Street's criminal culture that accompanies its "Mafia-like behavior"?

3. How much money do Wall Street companies have to spend to get a US politician to listen and be sympathetic to their cause, according to the author, citing Taibbi?

In a truly excellent, painstaking study, Mark Taibbi of *Rolling Stone* (of all magazines—really took my respect for RS up a few light years from an abysmal low where I considered it to be a poor relative of FOX News) wrote a very revealing and painstaking piece called "The Scam Wall Street Learned from the Mafia," about a court case (*USA v. Carollo*) that didn't get much play in mainstream media, partly because of its complexity and partly because of the "language barrier" of finance.

This relates to a very nasty range of banking practices from 2006, but it's like a How To manual for ripping off America's public money. It's a very long article, but if you're an American, this is compulsory reading, because this is where your taxes are going—straight into people's pockets. It also explains a lot about the very shifty behavior of American politicians of all stripes and at all levels.

## How Cities Raise Bonds

In a truly great bit of clear writing, Taibbi simplifies and explains the process of cities's raising bonds:

> In most cases, towns and cities, called issuers, are legally required to submit their bonds to a competitive auction of at

least three banks, called providers. The scam Wall Street cooked up to beat this fair-market system was to devise phony auctions. Instead of submitting competitive bids and letting the highest rate win, providers like Chase, Bank of America and GE [General Electric Capital Finance] secretly divvied up the business of all the different cities and towns that came to Wall Street to borrow money. One company would be allowed to "win" the bid on an elementary school, the second would be handed a hospital, the third a hockey rink, and so on.

By further skimming rates, the banks also collected a lot of extra money from their unwitting bankrollers. There was never any chance of the bonds getting a reasonable market rate. The banks would shave points off the returns. A fraction of a percentage point in this sort of money means millions in total, collected over years. Add up the number of municipal bonds on issue, and you get billions upon billions. There's no real estimate available, but Taibbi cites a few instances of proven admissions by the banks:

> Given the complexities of bond investments, it's impossible to know exactly how much the total take was. But consider this: Four banks that took part in the scam (UBS, Bank of America, Chase and Wells Fargo) paid $673 million in restitution after agreeing to cooperate in the government's case.

> (Chase paid just $75 million for its role in the bribe-and-payola scandal that saddled Jefferson County, Alabama, with more than $3 billion in sewer debt), it's safe to assume that Wall Street skimmed untold billions in the bid-rigging scam. The UBS settlement alone, for instance, involved 100 different bond deals, worth a total of $16 billion, over four years.

Fun, huh? Now *Bloomberg* on the same subject [in a July 2012 article by William D. Cohan], from yet another angle:

> For some reason, Wall Street never seems to get the message that bribing government officials—and paying each other

off—to get access to lucrative municipal-bond underwriting business is illegal. Wall Street has never learned this lesson because the miniscule price it ends up having to pay for misbehaving has absolutely no deterrent value whatsoever.

To put both articles another way, Wall Street pays peanuts for its crimes, if and when they're discovered. Any private citizen would get jail. The sacred bull of Wall Street, occasionally described by me as the Golden Calf that speaks at both ends, is literally aping well-known Mafia practices, targeting corrupt officials and rigging public contracts.

## An Accurate Analogy

The Mafia analogy is right on the money, excuse the pun. If you read [Italian writer and journalist] Roberto Saviano's literally death-defying major exposé of the Naples [Italy] organised crime groups generically called the Camorra, a truly startling book called *Gomorrah*, you won't need to be told how easy it is to simply go around laws and not get caught. Corruption is the key to successful organised crime.

The main difference between the banks and the Mafia is that they effectively have licenses to act the way they do. Only irrefutable evidence can get an actual indictment up and running, and that takes forever.

The Wall Street "culture" is the big problem.

In conjunction with the Mafia-like behavior, we have:

The revelations about Goldman Sachs [GS] and its "muppet" terminology for clients from retiring GS executive Greg Smith. This is rampant, and has been for years. I remember writing an article about some Wall Street brokerage firms which had "client-no-sue-us" clauses in their contracts for their clients. Meaning people couldn't even sue in defense of their own personal property.

The interesting coincidence that American cities are going broke by going guarantors for public works projects.

## Remaking the Definition of Crime

The terms "white-collar crime" and its offshoot, "organized crime," reflect a half-century-old movement to remake the very definition of crime. Professor Edwin Sutherland, a sociologist who coined the term "white-collar crime," disagreed with certain basic substantive and procedural principles of criminal law. In his landmark book, *White Collar Crime*, first published in 1949, Sutherland dismisses the traditional mens rea (criminal intent) requirement and the presumption of innocence. He suggests that the "rules of criminal intent and presumption of innocence . . . are not required in all prosecution in criminal courts and the number of exceptions authorized by statutes is increasing."

*John S. Baker, "The Sociological Origins of White-Collar Crime," Heritage Foundation, October 4, 2004.*

The finance sector's unholy effects on everything in American life from health insurance debt collection in ERs [emergency rooms] to college fees.

An intriguingly similar pattern in WalMart bribing Mexican officials.

This rabid money grubbing behavior is more or less according to the script of Saviano's book regarding the Camorra's foreign business in Europe, which includes everything from toxic waste "disposal", (meaning turning Naples into a garbage dump and poisoning the famous farmlands with dioxins, etc.) to syndicated multimillion-dollar pharmaceuticals scams. Never mind how many people get killed in the process. This is obsessive behavior and it's a dead ringer for the normal daily work of major organised crime groups.

## Buying Politicians

A few questions:

1. You have to wonder how so many financiers can so easily find and target so many corrupt people and get so many other people looking the other way.

2. Why is it that any form of law enforcement seems so hopelessly slow in tackling crimes which were obviously well known to thousands of people across hundreds of financial institutions?

3. How do financiers get so many reliably corrupt contacts? Because they're real "people" people, or because they know people who can find them?

4. How do US politicians seem to be so much in synch with so many people carrying out criminal activities on a routine basis for so long?

According to Taibbi, you can get the ear and perhaps more from a US politician for around 5 figures, even as low as $10,000. These guys aren't all Republicans, either. Former governor [of New Mexico] Bill Richardson was in trouble for alleged bribery under similar circumstances.

If you were to describe Wall Street as no more or less than the un-arrested Bernie Madoffs and Ken Lays [Wall Street businessmen indicted for fraud] of the moment, you'd be pretty right as a description but hopelessly optimistic in defining the problems.

These are scum. They're the biggest abusers of human rights and property on Earth. They've thoroughly trashed the US economy, crippled Middle America, and destroyed any number of millions of lives. There is no possible reason within the bounds of any sort of honest logic for protecting the finance sector from the law. Yet successive Congresses and successive administrations have failed to do one single solitary thing to deal with this problem.

## The Plague of White Collar Crime

This is a true social disease, and it's been spreading for a long time. It's been "syphilis of the soul" for the American way of life. First the balls go, then the brain. Al Capone died of it. Prior to the 1980s, there were no billionaire criminals. Organized crime made more money as movies than in real life. White collar crime, apart from some comparatively very low level scams, was a new idea.

These guys simply can't be making that sort of money out of mere drug deals and people smuggling. They also go where the money is, and that money has been in finance since the 1980s. The disease is now a plague, actively encouraged by a toxic anti-human culture which simply doesn't obey laws on principle. This methodology is quite safe. Banks can rip off people for billions, and at no real penalty. It's like giving parking fines to mass murderers.

Some more honest logic—

Those who do not enforce the law or actively prevent enforcement are effectively aiding and abetting organised crime. Is this collusion? It sure as hell looks like it. It's Christmas for Wall Street every day.

I hate to paraphrase this sacred phrase this way, but what else could you call it—

"Government of the criminals, by the criminals, for the criminals."

... Because government obviously isn't working for anyone else anymore, even in theory.

# Periodical and Internet Sources Bibliography

*The following articles have been selected to supplement the diverse views presented in this chapter.*

| | |
|---|---|
| Tom Beil | "A Dangerous Game," *Chemistry and Industry*, July 2013. |
| Daniel Grushkin | "The New Highway Robbery," *Bloomberg Businessweek*, May 30, 2011. |
| Timothy R. Hawthorne | "Why Counterfeiting Hurts," *Response*, January 2012. |
| Rebecca Lowe | "War on Fakes," *IBA Global Insight*, August/September 2013. |
| Vishak Raman | "Cybercrime-as-a-Service—a Very Modern Business," *PC Quest*, March 2013. |
| Mark Schoofs | "ATMs Become Handy Tool for Laundering Dirty Cash," *Wall Street Journal*, September 21, 2007. |
| Daniel Sheinis | "The Links Between Human Trafficking, Organized Crime, and Terrorism," *American Intelligence Journal*, March 2012. |
| Octavia Steriopol, Luciana Boboc, and Varvara Coman | "The Trafic of Human Beings Is Inhuman," *Contemporary Readings in Law and Social Justice*, 2012. |
| Michael White and Nora Zimmett | "Organized Crime Goes to the Movies," *Bloomberg Businessweek*, April 11, 2011. |

OPPOSING
VIEWPOINTS®
SERIES

CHAPTER 3

What Policies Should Be
Implemented to Address
Organized Crime?

# Chapter Preface

In the United States, a chief statutory weapon against organized crime is the Racketeer Influenced and Corrupt Organizations Act (RICO) of 1970. The act stemmed from a presidential commission on crime in the late 1960s, and the need for the act as well as its sweeping scope derived from an overriding belief that a united criminal network had pervaded the nation and had infiltrated legitimate business. Indeed, much of the wording in the initial bill makes the assumption that a single criminal syndicate was threatening public interest. By the time the act was passed in Congress, the wording was expanded to indict not a specific criminal entity but various manifestations of criminal enterprise. The final RICO statutes, then, targeted any operation that carried the taint of corruption or racketeering by defining what a criminal organization does rather than clarifying its composition.

The significance of RICO, however, lay not in defining a group whose criminal activities warranted prosecution but in permitting law enforcement to implicate the entire hierarchy of a criminal enterprise in the wrongdoing of any of its members. That is, anyone who invested in a criminal activity might be subject to prosecution, and leaders of criminal organizations could be indicted for the crimes committed by their subordinates. As part of the act reads, "It shall be unlawful for any person who has received any income derived, directly or indirectly, from a pattern of racketeering activity or through collection of an unlawful debt in which such person has participated as a principal . . . , to use or invest, directly or indirectly, any part of such income, or the proceeds of such income, in acquisition of any interest in, or the establishment or operation of, any enterprise which is engaged in, or the activities of which affect, interstate or foreign commerce." The broad language allowed law enforcement to go after Mafia chiefs, for example, even if these leaders never soiled their own hands in the day-to-day criminal affairs that keep their organizations funded. In addition, RICO can be used to chart a pattern of criminal activity. As Nathan Koppel writes in a January 2011 article for the *Wall Street Journal*, "The law allows federal prosecutors to stitch together crimes going back many years, from extortion and loan sharking to murder, in a single case."

The broad reach of RICO led to several prosecutions of notorious Mafia crime families in the 1980s, proving that the structure of the organizations could be toppled by indicting various foot soldiers and linking their activities to those higher up in the chain of command. Many federal prosecutors were pleased with the results they were able to achieve in cracking tight-knit organizations like the mob. Some observers, though, were less congratulatory when the loose prose of the act was turned against labor unions and legal businesses. In a March 1990 article in *Reason* magazine, L. Gordon Crovitz notes that accusations of mail fraud and wire fraud have been used to launch federal investigations of groups that seemingly had no connection to organized crime. While instances of mail fraud or wire fraud had traditionally fallen under the purview of civil or local law, RICO opened the door to federal prosecution. Citing American jurists, Crovitz contends that the notion of fraud is so vague that it invites misapplication. Coupled with the fact that "these days almost no business is conducted without letters, faxes, or modems," Crovitz argues that "nearly any allegation of 'fraud' can become a RICO case." Thus, he states, RICO became a weapon used against bankers and brokers who may have committed a violation but who incurred federal prosecution because they are popularly conceived of as wealthy scofflaws rather than criminal syndicates.

The RICO statutes have remained a prominent tool in the US arsenal against organized crime. In the following chapter, several authors debate the value and legitimacy of other policies that law enforcement and government have implemented (or considered implementing) in the struggle to curb related illegal activities.

"*The fact is that the current drug laws
are contributing to an all-out war on
our southern border.*"

# Legalizing Marijuana Would Weaken the Drug Cartels

*Gary Johnson*

*In the viewpoint that follows, Gary Johnson argues that the
United States needs to reexamine its policies on drugs in America,
particularly marijuana laws, which he claims are contributing to
violence and corruption in the United States and Mexico.
Johnson argues that Mexican leaders have realized that their
drug policies are not working, but he says that US leaders, including President Barack Obama, refuse to admit this fact.
Johnson contends that the money from marijuana sales in the
States could be regulated and taxed but instead goes into the
pockets of drug cartels. Only through legalization would these
problems be overcome and the flow of money to the cartels
stopped. Gary Johnson has been a Libertarian Party presidential
candidate and is the former governor of New Mexico.*

As you read, consider the following questions:

1. According to the author, what percentage of the Mexican drug cartels' revenue comes from selling marijuana in the United States?

2. Johnson cites US researcher Jon Gettman, who estimates that the illegal sale of drugs in America is an industry that earns how much money a year for criminals?

3. Johnson compares today's prohibition on marijuana to alcohol prohibition in the 1920s and finds what similarities?

There were 72 bodies found on a ranch ninety miles south of the Texas border—obvious victims of a drug cartel massacre. Bullets have been hitting public buildings in El Paso and the *Washington Post* is reporting that at least $20 billion a year in cash is being smuggled across the U.S. border each year. What is it going to take to convince the Federal Government that current drug policies are not working? The fact is that the current drug laws are contributing to an all-out war on our southern border—all in the name of a modern-day prohibition that is no more logical or realistic than the one we abandoned 75 years ago?

## Cartels Get Rich on Illegal Drugs

Mexican drug cartels make at least 60 percent of their revenue from selling marijuana in the United States, according to the White House Office of National Drug Control Policy. The FBI estimates that the cartels now control distribution in more than 230 American cities, from the Southwest to New England.

How are they able to do this? Because America's policy for almost 70 years has been to keep marijuana—arguably no more harmful than alcohol and used by 15 million Americans every month—confined to the illicit market, meaning we've given criminals a virtual monopoly on something that U.S. researcher Jon Gettman estimates is a $36 billion a year industry, greater than corn and wheat combined. We have implemented laws that are not enforceable, which has thereby created a thriving black market. By denying reality and not regulating and taxing marijuana, we are fueling not only this massive illicit economy, but a war that we are clearly losing.

In 2006, Mexican president Felipe Calderón announced a new military offensive against his country's drug cartels. Since then, more than 28,000 people have been killed in prohibition-fueled violence, and the cartels are more powerful than ever, financed primarily by marijuana sales. Realizing that his hardline approach has not worked, earlier this month [August 2010] Calderón said the time has come for Mexico to have an open debate about regulating drugs as a way to combat the cartels. Ignoring this problem, Mr. Calderón said, "is an unacceptable option."

Calderon's predecessor, Vicente Fox, went even further, writing on his blog that "we should consider legalizing the production, sale and distribution of drugs" as a way to "weaken and break the economic system that allows cartels to earn huge profits . . . Radical prohibition strategies have never worked."

Fox is not alone. His predecessor, as well as former presidents of Brazil and Colombia, has also spoken out for the need to end prohibition.

And they're right. Crime was rampant during alcohol prohibition as well. Back then it was led by gangsters like Al Capone. Now it's led by cartels.

The violence in Mexico is out of control and is destroying the country. Journalists fear reporting the daily shootouts because of threats from the cartels. Some schools are even teaching their students to duck and cover in order to avoid the crossfire. Politicians are being targeted for assassination.

## Legalizing Marijuana in California Would Hurt the Mexican Drug Cartels

Mexican DTOs [drug trafficking organizations] earn $1.1 billion to $2 billion from exporting marijuana to the U.S. and selling it to wholesalers across the southwest border. Legalizing marijuana in California would present two sources of competition. The obvious one is marijuana sold legally in California to California residents and drug "tourists" visiting from out of state, as well as legalized home cultivation. A less obvious but potentially more important threat is marijuana diverted from legal distribution channels. The latter includes marijuana that is grown legally in California but then smuggled to another state and sold illegally there, as well as marijuana sold to underage users in California.

We believe that legalizing marijuana in California would effectively eliminate Mexican DTOs' revenues from supplying Mexican grown marijuana to the California market. . . . Even with taxes, legally produced marijuana would likely cost no more than would illegal marijuana from Mexico and would cost less than half as much per unit of THC [tetrahydrocannabinol]. Thus, the needs of the California market would be supplied by the new legal industry. While, in theory, some DTO employees might choose to work in the legal marijuana industry, they would not be able to generate unusual profits, nor be able to draw on talents that are particular to a criminal organization.

*Beau Kilmer, Jonathan P. Caulkins, Brittany M. Bond, and Peter H. Reuter, "Reducing Drug Trafficking Revenues and Violence in Mexico: Would Legalizing Marijuana in California Help?," RAND Corporation, 2010. wwww.rand.com*

## The Violence Has Spread

The havoc has spread into the United States. In March [2010], hit men executed three people linked to the U.S. Consulate in Juarez, an act that President [Barack] Obama condemned. And the same cartels that are selling marijuana in the United States are destroying treasured environmental resources by growing marijuana illegally in protected park lands. By regulating marijuana, such illegal grows would cease to exist. The problem has been out of hand for quite some time, and a new approach is desperately needed.

Sadly, U.S. officials refuse to even acknowledge that such a debate is taking place. Drug Czar Gil Kerlikowske has said repeatedly that the Obama administration is not open to a debate on ending marijuana prohibition. Even worse, we've continued to fund Mexico's horribly failed drug war (to the tune of $ 1.4 billion through the Mérida Initiative), while refusing to be honest with our neighbors who are urgently seeking a new direction.

This November [2010], Californians will decide whether to legalize marijuana for adults 21 and older [which was defeated]. U.S. officials need to welcome the debate on marijuana regulation. It's probably the only practical way to weaken the drug cartels—something both the U.S. and Mexico would benefit from immeasurably. We need a new solution to stop this violence.

> "Although frequently portrayed as an effective solution to the problem of organized crime, mere legalization . . . of drugs, is no panacea."

# Organized Criminals Won't Fade Away

*Vanda Felbab-Brown*

*In the following viewpoint, Vanda Felbab-Brown argues that legalization of drugs alone will not stop organized criminals from controlling the drug trade. Felbab-Brown asserts that the United States is in fact safer than other countries, like Mexico, from drug violence because of its strict enforcement of drug laws. Felbab-Brown says that what is needed is not legalization but better drug policies that involve the communities and focus on reducing violence. Felbab-Brown is a Fellow in Foreign Policy at the Brookings Institution, a Washington, DC, think tank, and is the author of many works on illicit economies and organized crime.*

As you read, consider the following questions:

1. What does the author say characterizes the US drug market today?

Vanda Felbab-Brown, "Organized Criminals Won't Fade Away," *World Today*, vol. 68, no. 12, August 2012. Copyright © 2012 by The Royal Institute of International Affairs. All rights reserved. Reproduced by permission.

2. According to Felbab-Brown, why would a government tax on legal drugs help organized criminals who sell drugs?

3. What does the author identify as an appropriate anti-crime response?

Policies that focus on suppressing drug flows are often ineffective in suppressing organized crime. Under the worst circumstances, such as in Mexico or Afghanistan, policing policies, such as high-value targeting or eradication of illicit crops, can trigger intense criminal violence or strengthen insurgencies. But neither is legalization an effective shortcut to law enforcement. On its own, it is unlikely to address a host of problems associated with organized crime.

Illicit economies exist in some form virtually everywhere. For example, some part of the illegal drug economy—production, trafficking, or distribution—is present in almost every country. Although the drug trade is widely believed to be the most profitable illicit economy, dwarfing others such as the illegal trade in wildlife or logging, its impact on society and the intensity of violence and corruption it generates vary in different regions and over time.

Like Colombia in the 1980s, Mexico today is blighted by violence. But although many of the same drug trafficking groups operate in both Mexico and the United States, their behaviour is strikingly different north of the border where their capacity to corrupt state institutions is limited and the level of violence they generate is small.

Indeed, what characterizes the US drug market today—most of which operates behind closed doors, off the streets, and over the Internet—is how peaceful it is. Such variation is found in other contexts too: the Yakuza, even while dominating the construction economy in Japan, is far less violent than Hong Kong's Tongs or Latin America's organized crime.

Many things account for the variation in violence, including demographic factors, such as the age of criminal capos [heads] and the geographic concentration of minority groups, levels of poverty, the balance of power in the criminal market as well as the capacity of policing agencies and their choice of strategies. Beyond violence, the strength and presence of the state are critical in determining the impact of illicit markets on society.

Organized crime has a particularly vicious impact on the state if it can create strong bonds with larger segments of the population than the state can. Many people around the world in areas with an inadequate or problematic state presence, great poverty, and social and political marginalization are dependent on illicit economies for their livelihood.

Criminal (as well as militant) groups provide the marginalized population with employment and an opportunity for social advancement. They can also provide a level of security, suppressing robberies, thefts, kidnapping, and murders as well as providing informal courts, despite their being instigators of crime and instability in the first place. As a result, criminal entities can gain political capital with local communities.

Although frequently portrayed as an effective solution to the problem of organized crime, mere legalization of illicit economies, particularly of drugs, is no panacea.

Proponents of legalization as a mechanism to reduce organized crime make at least two arguments: it will severely deprive organized crime groups of resources. It will also free law enforcement agencies to concentrate on other types of crime.

A country may have good reasons to want to legalize the use and even production of some addictive substances and ride out the consequences of greater use. Such reasons could include providing better health care to users, reducing the number of users in prison, and perhaps even generating greater revenues and giving jobs to the poor.

## Prohibition of Drugs Leads to Human Rights Violations

Unveiling the role of moral entrepreneurs and the weight of economic interests in discourses that shaped the drugs shift from commodities to evildoers, . . . has evidenced how rising claims for control and stringent law enforcement have culminated with the so-called "war on drugs", irrespective of the human rights violations that it creates. Strategies for fighting drugs targeted the supply side of the drug market, and are especially disadvantageous to producing countries, which tend also to be developing countries with less leverage than consuming countries (United States and Europe, according to UNODC [United Nations Office on Drugs and Crime]) at global decision-making fora.

Brazilian estimates on drug-related homicide provide a glimpse into how developing countries tied to the global drug market are burdened with drug-related harm, such as high drug-related homicide rates, and a distinct lack of resources for the basic provision of human dignity. Analysis of those features suggests that UNODC policies have been overly concerned with crop eradication and drugs seizure. It also suggests that, certainly in human rights terms, the prohibitionist approach is not evidence-based, and on the contrary, creates conditions for abuses by denying their cause-effect relationship with prohibition itself.

*Fernanda Mena and Dick Hobbs, "Narcophobia: Drugs, Prohibition and the Generation of Human Rights Abuses," Trends in Organized Crime, March 2010.*

Yet without robust state presence and effective law enforcement, both often elusive in parts of the world such as

Latin America or Africa, there can be little assurance that organized crime groups would be excluded from the legal drug trade. In fact, they may have numerous advantages over legal companies and manage to hold on to the trade, perhaps even resorting to violence to do so. Nor does mere legalization mean that the state will suddenly become robust and effective. Persistent deficiencies in the state explain why there is so much illegal logging alongside legal logging, for example, or why smuggling in legal goods take place.

Organized crime groups who stand to be displaced from the drug trade by legalization can hardly be expected to take the change lying down. Rather, they may intensify their violent power struggles over remaining illegal economies, such as the smuggling of other contraband or migrants, prostitution, extortion, and kidnapping. To mitigate their financial losses, they may also seek to take over the black economy, which operates outside the tax system. If they succeed in organizing street life in this informal sector, their political power over society will be greater than ever.

Nor does legalization imply that police would be freed up to focus on other issues or become less corrupt: The state may have to devote more resources to regulating the legal economy.

Additionally, a grey market in drugs would probably emerge. If drugs became legal, the state would want to tax them—to generate revenues and to discourage greater use. The higher the tax, the greater the opportunity for organized crime to undercut the state by charging less. Organized crime groups could set up their own fields with smaller taxation, snatch the market and the profits, and the state would be back to combating them and eradicating their fields. Such grey markets exist alongside a host of legal economies, from cigarettes to stolen cars.

Without capable and accountable police that are responsive to the needs of the people and are backed-up by an efficient, accessible, and transparent justice system, the state cannot manage either legal or illegal economies.

Reducing the violence associated with drug trafficking should be a priority for police. Governments that effectively reduce the violence surrounding illicit economies often may not be able to *rid* their countries of organized crime; they can, however, lessen its grip on society, thereby giving their people greater confidence in government, encouraging citizen cooperation with law enforcement, and aiding the transformation of a national security threat into a public safety problem. That can happen—and many countries have succeeded in doing so—in the absence of legalization.

An appropriate anti-crime response is a multifaceted statebuilding effort that seeks to strengthen the bonds between the state and marginalized communities dependent on or vulnerable to participation in illicit economies. Efforts need to focus on ensuring that communities will obey laws—by increasing the likelihood that illegal behaviour and corruption will be punished via effective law enforcement, but also by creating a social, economic, and political environment in which the laws are consistent with the needs of the people.

> "The legal, responsible gun owner is mainly responsible for arming up the gangs of America."

# Better Gun Control Would Reduce Gang-Related Violence

*Tiffany Willis*

*Tiffany Willis asserts in the following viewpoint that the main way that gang members acquire guns is by stealing them or buying them from legal gun owners. She argues that due to these facts, legal gun owners are partially responsible for gang shootings. Willis points to various facts showing that gang violence is a huge problem in America, particularly among minorities. Willis maintains that it is the responsibility of legal gun owners to lock up their guns and to not sell legal weapons at gun shows. Willis founded the website Liberal America and counts herself a proud member of the Christian Left.*

As you read, consider the following questions:

1. Willis states that gang violence accounts for what percentage of all violent crime in America?

Tiffany Willis, "Who Arms America's Gangs?: Responsible Gun Owners," LiberalAmerica .org, May 27, 2013. Copyright © 2013 by Tiffany Willis. All rights reserved. Reproduced by permission.

2. The author cites a Nashville news story that quoted gang member Jonathan Gutierrez as saying that he acquired his guns where?

3. The author argues that criminals do not buy guns retail but get them in what other ways?

When we talk about death by gun violence, it is very easy to fall into one of two traps: [to] either cover all gun violence deaths under the same blanket or to only look at the results of gun violence from those types that are media friendly. Gun violence comes from a myriad of sources; from kids finding daddy's gun to spree killing to mass murder to domestic violence to gang violence. Solutions cannot be found under one blanket, where one size fits all—the solutions, and the causes of the problems are disparate, and from that we look at the different types of gun violence that results in death.

Gang violence has been a part of this country's history since the early 1800s, from the early Irish gangs of New York, where it was estimated that 55,000 immigrants held allegiance to gangs in 1855 (out of a total population of 550,000) to the Italian gangs that began in the early 20th Century and the rise of small gangs during Prohibition. American history, both academic and popular, is riddled with the famous and their Hollywood counterparts, intertwined—[Al] Capone, [Carlo] Gambino, Bonnie and Clyde, Lucky Luciano, *Godfather*, *Goodfellas*, *Sopranos*.

They have splintered further—Crips, Bloods, Latin Kings, Devil's Disciples, Vice Lords, and Triads. They cross every ethnic line, from Irish to Italian to Mexican to Russian; white, black, Latino, Asian.

## A Big Problem in America

That brings us to the 21st century. Gangs are represented by nearly all ethnic groups, by drug cartels, by the disenfranchised, and the mean. It is reported that gang violence accounts for over 50% of *all* violent crime in this country. The FBI reports that 800 murders are committed by gangs, both "gangland" and juvenile gangs each year. Another 800 murders are committed by drug interactions. All in all, about 15% of the 10,000 murders are committed with guns in this country.

So, where do gang members get their guns? With many having some criminal record and their names flagged on NICS [National Instant Criminal Background Check System], how do the estimated 1,400,000 gang members in this country get armed up?

## Gangs Get Guns from Legal Owners

Turns out, the legal, responsible gun owner is mainly responsible for arming up the gangs of America. How? Several ways, including, but not limited to leaving guns unlocked that get stolen (about 240,000 each year) to selling them at gun shows and on the Internet to those who have cash in hand, and where no questions are asked.

Earlier this month [May 2013, TV station] WTVF Nashville completed an investigative report of gang members in jail and how they got their weapons. Jonathan Gutierrez, serving a life sentence for murder in Tennessee, when asked where he got his guns told reporters, "Most of the weapons that were used were coming from the gun show." Further, he said that at age 15, he and other gang members went to local gun shows with cash and were easily able to buy four to six guns each visit.

"Anybody will sell you a gun," Gutierrez said. "I mean no matter what, if you want a gun and you show them the money, and tell them you want to buy it, he's going to definitely sell it to you."

Now, does this mean we blame the gun owners for the violence that those guns in the hands of criminals do? Not directly—but gun owners do hand a lot of weapons to gang members.

## Organized Crime and Gun Violence

Whether investigating an illicit transnational drug trafficking market or a criminal group involved in cross-border gun trafficking, investigators are increasingly recognizing that illicit markets and criminal groups are closely associated with guns and violence. Firearms and their related materials, such as ammunition, can have two significant roles. They can be (a) the primary commodity of the market itself, or (b) the instruments that are relied upon by the criminal groups to exert the physical force required to direct and sustain their illicit markets.

The misuse of firearms by criminals operating within illicit markets clearly results in injury and death—not only to the confederates involved but to innocent bystanders as well. Society must act on behalf of these victims to stop armed criminals before they can shoot and kill again.

Working with the belief that "every crime gun has a story to tell," law enforcement benefits by taking a "presumptive approach" to the investigation of crimes involving the misuse of firearms.

*Pete Gagliardi, "Organized Crime Is Often*
*Tied to Gun Trafficking and Gun Violence,"*
International Review of Law, Computers and Technology,
*March 2012.*

Put another way, if, every year you handed 240,000 guns to five-year-olds and left them unsupervised, *they* would be responsible for pulling the trigger, but it would be that person that made the gun available who would hold ultimate responsibility. The same goes for those who sell guns without background checks, who sell them to straw purchasers, who don't lock up their weapons and have them stolen. With every right comes responsibility. And, like it or not, it is our responsibility as gun owners to make sure *our* weapons do not end up in the hands of criminals.

We have to face the facts that criminals don't buy retail. They steal guns, they buy stolen guns, they buy perfectly legal guns from "responsible" gun owners at gun shows, they use straw purchasers to buy guns, and they buy from federally licensed dealers who know that the chance of the ATF [Bureau of Alcohol, Tobacco, Firearms, and Explosives] inspecting them is near zero because of ATF budgets. They know the weaknesses in the system and they exploit them. And we as a nation pay dearly for that in loss of life, in costs for emergency rooms, and in law enforcement costs associated with the thousands of deaths and injuries each and every year because of illegal guns.

But the saddest part of this, gun owners blow it off, ignore the responsibility that they hold, refuse to tighten the filters, making it harder for criminals to get guns. Gun owners have said they don't want to be bothered with the ten minute background check that would be helpful, and they don't feel it is their responsibility to lock up their weapons away from criminals, and away from kids. So the deaths will continue as long as "responsible" gun owners prove yet again that they really are not.

> *"Ban guns? . . . We will then have gang wars only Hollywood [special effects] departments can envision."*

# Banning Guns Will Increase Gang-Related Violence

*Michael Geer*

*In the following viewpoint, Michael Geer argues that gun violence should be blamed not on legal gun owners but on gangs, because most violent crime in the United States is perpetrated by gang members, not by legal gun owners. Further, he asserts that if gun ownership is made illegal in the United States in an attempt to halt this violence, gang members will still acquire guns illegally, but the average person will have no way of defending themselves against criminals. Michael Geer is a blogger, author, publisher, and a contributor to* American Thinker.

As you read, consider the following questions:

1. According to the statistics cited by Geer, what percentage of cities with a population greater than 250,000 reported gang activity in 2001?

2. What does Geer blame for creating "an industry with such disregard for the law to be staggering in depth and breadth"?

3. What does the author claim would happen if the United
   States banned guns?

Guns and gangs. Haven't read anything from the Left about
that. Certainly nothing from Congress. But with FBI statistics showing more than 1,500,000 members of recognized
gangs across the nation and something like 33,000 recognized
gangs in the FBI's stats, you'd think Gun Control advocates
would list these as a major target of their efforts, especially
since gang activity is responsible for at least 18% of criminal
and violent activity throughout the US.

You'd be wrong.

Stats:

100% of cities with populations greater than or equal to
250,000 reported gang activity in 2001

85% of cities with populations between 100,000 and
229,999 reported gang activity in 2001

65% of cities with populations between 50,000 and 99,999
reported gang activity in 2001

44% of cities with populations between 25,000 and 49,999
reported gang activity in 2001

20% of cities with populations between 2,500 and 24,999
reported gang activity in 2001

35% of suburban counties reported gang activity in 2001

11% of rural counties reported gang activity in 2001

95% of the jurisdictions reporting gang activity in 2001
had also reported gang activity in previous survey years

3,000 jurisdictions across the US are estimated to have had
gang activity in 2001

56% of cities with populations greater than or equal to 100,000 reported an increase or no significant change in the number of gang members in 2001

42% of cities with a population of at least 25,000 reported an increase in the number of gang members

45% of cities with a population of at least 25,000 reported an increase in the number of gangs from the previous two years

69% of cities with populations of at least 100,000 reported having gang-related homicides in 2001

37% of cities with populations between 50,000 and 99,999 reported having gang-related homicides in 2001

59% of all homicides in 2001 in Los Angeles and

53% in Chicago were gang related; there was a total of 698 gang-related homicides in these two cities combined, whereas 130 other cities with populations of at least 100,000 with gang problems reported having a total of 637 homicides among them

Reports about you and me and our AR-15s and AKs [assault rifles]? All over the front page. Gangs with rocket launchers and grenades in the gun control newspeak? Bupkus [nothing]. You and I and our Glocks [handguns]? Terrified reporters breathless with passion for gun control. Gangs with Glocks? Nada [nothing]. You and I, presuming you may be religious, a veteran of armed service or a defender of the Second Amendment, are now listed with Homeland Security as a threat to National Security, a potential terrorist. Lumped in there with the likes of [militant Islamist group] Hamas, [Peruvian Communist rebels] Shining Path, [Salvadoran gang] MS-13 and [biker gang] the Hells Angels. But right now we're not hearing anything about trying to take guns away from the Mongols. No. You're not hearing some rip-and-read talking head demanding MS-13 be disarmed. You and me, yes. Insanely violent drug gangs? Shhh. No gun control for them, they might do something.

## Gang Members Will Always Have Guns

Very few members of gangs walk our streets minus a gun. From renegade motorcycle gangs to inner city street gangs to international cartel gang members, every one of them is strapped. We don't need footnoted statistics to know the truth of that.

Criminal gangs are already engaging in criminal activity, meaning, they have no problem breaking the Law. Breaking the Law is their way of life. The punitive measures of Law meant to cause prior self-restraint mean nothing to them. Consequences mean almost nothing to them.

Gun Control advocates are terrified of the average Mom and Dad, the average brother or sister possessing the means to defend themselves and those around them. They don't seem at all worried about armed members of gangs. At least they never volunteer to go disarm them.

Gangs don't care about Law. They don't care about the consequences of breaking a Law. But let me tell you what they do care about. You shooting back. Put a couple rounds of 185-grain .45 ACP in them, or past their head, that's a consequence they understand. When you drop a gang aggressor like third period French, that's a consequence they understand.

Law? Not so much.

So, let's say Congress passes enough gun control war-garble that in effect it is impossible to possess and use a firearm. Will gang members remain disarmed as the rest of the sheeple?

(that's me, laughing)

Gangs get guns as a result of criminal activity. Burglaries, theft, selling drugs to buy guns on the street, all manner of illegally obtaining guns. You and me? Federally licensed fire-arms dealer, background check, traceable funds, paperwork, etc.

The criminal element will always get access because they have no regard for Law. You and I do our best to obey Laws because we dare not entertain the consequences of breaking the Law.

Which brings us to the question of follow the money, always the ultimate driving force.

Prohibition produced the potent opportunity for unthinkable fortunes that funded vast gang networks that exist to this day. People wanted liquor despite the nanny-staters in Congress and people got liquor. Through violent gangs which profited to such an extent they destabilized governments. They blackmailed, killed, murdered, through bribing, extortion, threatening and quite literally waging war on the Law and anyone who stood in their way. Gang wars and gang profits produced enough profit to fuel the violence with serious automatic weapons, explosives and murder for hire.

The rootstock of many of those gangs are still with us. Look at Chicago.

The War on Drugs has produced an industry with such disregard for Law to be staggering in depth and breadth. It isn't just Colombia. It's not just hyper-violent Mexican drug cartels. It's not just Chicago. Think opium fields in Afghanistan and how many of our servicemen and women have died there. Think Beqaa Valley [Lebanon] and perpetual violence. Think drug warlords deep in the Shan Mountains of SE Asia. There is so much money to be made in prohibited drugs there are no words adequate to describe it.

And none of these players obey the Law. Laws in their thousands in every nation, yet the money flows and laws are broken and gangs thrive. Only the law abiding suffer.

## Banning Guns Will Worsen the Problem

But, ban guns? Make a new Prohibition in effect negating the Second Amendment? You think we have a gang problem now? You think extant gangs will ignore the eye popping opportunity banning guns and ammunition will represent? We already have a serious nationwide gang problem. Congress will corrupt that minor problem into what could become a destabilizing all out conflagration.

We will then have gang wars only Hollywood [special effects] departments can envision. Not because you and I will go hog wild ignoring the Law. But because Nature abhors a vacuum. And gangs already exist and which already disregard the Law will—go hog wild stepping into the natural Supply and Demand cycle.

Gangs and Guns. I really would like to see [gun control advocates Senator] Dianne Feinstein and [political commentator] Ed Schultz go to addresses in the Pico-Union area of Los Angeles and forcibly insist MS-13 members hand over their guns.

I really would.

Gangs are a huge problem Congress ignores. And I have to ask the question: if I follow the money, will I discover why? Because no decent law abiding self-respecting power center would allow gangs like these to exist in their body except that there were a reason to tolerate their presence. If we follow the money will we uncover why violent gangs are allowed to coexist side by side with decent law abiding citizens?

Feinstein ignores gangs and focuses on you. Think it through.

> "Cooperation between organized crime and terrorist groups should lead to governments and law enforcement agencies developing assertive and coordinated counter-strategies."

# The Crime-Terrorism Nexus

*Wibke Hansen*

*In the viewpoint that follows, Wibke Hansen explains that there are various and complex ways in which organized crime and terrorism coexist and contends that in order to combat these threats, these connections must be clearly defined and addressed through a concerted international effort. She maintains that the relationship between organized crime and terrorism can be defined in three ways—coexistence, cooperation, and confluence—each describing an increased level of interaction between the two, often taking place in states with weak governments. Hansen contends that these varying connections between terrorists and organized crime require a cooperative effort between governments and law enforcement agencies worldwide to develop coordinated counter-strategies to combat organized crime and terrorism in weakened states. Hansen is head of analysis and the deputy director of the Center for International Peace Operations.*

As you read, consider the following questions:

1. Hansen says that organized crime in fragile or post-conflict states can do what?

2. What does the author identify as the most important reason why organized criminals and terrorists sometimes will not work together?

3. The author asserts that when terrorists become increasingly involved in commercial enterprises, what occurs?

Organized crime (OC) is associated with a range of security threats, including kidnapping, human trafficking, organ trafficking, and outright violence. By facilitating the circulation of weapons, drugs, counterfeit pharmaceuticals and other smuggled goods, organized crime also poses indirect but more widespread threats to security.

In some cases, organized crime can also undermine states themselves. While Europol's 2007 Organised Crime Threat Assessment stressed that such groups do not pose a direct threat to Europol member states, this is not the case for less resilient, fragile or post-conflict states. Here, OC can erode state structures, undermine the rule of law, reduce the legitimacy of governments and widen the gap between citizens and state institutions.

The threat from organized crime, however, takes on another dimension when linked with groups that violently oppose the state, be they guerillas, rebels or terrorist groups. Among Western policy-makers, the assessment of organized crime as a security threat changes dramatically when linked to transnational terrorism.

Intersections between terrorism and OC can be divided into three broad categories: co-existence, cooperation and confluence. The organized crime–terrorism nexus may consist of interactions between separate entities—where each is engaged in essentially different activities—as well as occur within one entity involved in different types of criminal behavior.

## Coexistence

Coexistence refers to situations where organized criminals and terrorist groups operate in the same theatre but explicitly remain separate entities. And while there is no cooperation between the groups, their combined presence can generate cumulative effects. A RAND study from 2007 on terrorism in ungoverned territories suggests that factors including infrastructure, operational access, favorable social characteristics and the presence of sources of income contribute to a territory's attractiveness to terrorist groups. And while business opportunities tend to be the overriding consideration for organized crime groups, an adequate infrastructure, market access and reduced risk of detection are also important.

Although fragile states do not attract organized crime and terrorist activities per se, both groups benefit from weak state structures, particularly in areas such as border control and law enforcement. Both also require certain types of infrastructure and services for their operations. Ultimately, both OC and terrorists benefit from populations accustomed to seeking goods and services from non-state suppliers and which have developed a degree of tolerance for illicit business activities.

Accordingly, some of the features that make an environment conducive to organized crime also make it attractive to terrorist groups. Where terrorist groups and organized crime are both present, they will share an interest in maintaining the most appealing social, economic and political features of that environment. As a result, their combined presence can heighten the threat to state structures even if they do not explicitly act together.

## Cooperation

For cooperation between terrorist and criminal groups to occur, the gains for both partners have to overcome inherent obstacles and outweigh the risks. There are a number of reasons why organized crime and terrorist groups do *not* cooperate with each other. Most important of these are differences in motives.[1] Terrorist groups pursue political agendas whereas organized criminals tend to seek changes to the political status quo only when it threatens their activities. And while the profit to be made from illicit activities is the primary motivation for organized criminals, terrorists regard profit making ventures as a means rather than an end.

Consequently, as both groups seek to protect their operations, collaboration with outside actors—with different motives, ideologies or cultural dispositions—is inherently risky. It can also result in increased attention from law-enforcement agencies. However, the benefits of cooperation can outweigh these risks where certain goods or services—or specific types of operational support—can be acquired in a cost-effective manner from the other type of group. In some cases, customer-service provider relationships have developed, as both criminals and terrorist groups often require similar expertise, support structures and services—including false papers, IT [information technology] and communications specialists, and counter-surveillance technology.

## Confluence

A different type of customer-service provider relationship can occur where one group controls territory which is of strategic value for the operational goals of the other. This could include the taxing of illicit revenue streams or the provision of protection or transport for a share of the profits. However, despite opportunities for cooperation, most analysts agree that long-term alliances between OC and terrorist groups are unlikely. Where it does occur, cooperation is more likely to be ad-hoc, short-term and focused upon specific operational requirements. While the pooling of resources and assets between the two types of groups is conceivable, it requires very long-term arrangements to be reliable.

## Organized Crime Could Supply Terrorists with Nukes

The real threat of nuclear terrorism stems from the world's growing stock-piles of plutonium and HEU [highly enriched uranium], both of which can be used to make crude atomic bombs. . . .

Until recently, insiders who illicitly obtained fissile material were regularly arrested; they knew what to steal but not how to sell it. Over the past several years, however, organized crime groups in the Black Sea area appear to have become involved in nuclear smuggling. Their knowledge of smuggling tactics and poor coordination among local law enforcement agencies make it likely that—unless the United States significantly steps up its law enforcement efforts in the region—terrorists will eventually be able to buy enough fissile material to make at least a crude atomic device.

*Bruce Lawlor,*
*"The Black Sea: Center of the Nuclear Black Market,"*
Bulletin of the Atomic Scientists, 2011.

A nexus between organized crime and terrorism, however, does not require separate organizations. In fact, its most common form might be the confluence of both types of activity within one entity. Organized criminal networks have long used terror tactics to safeguard business interests and protect their working environments. Indeed, the term "narcoterrorism" was originally coined to refer to precisely this phenomenon. More significant, however, is the recent cultivation of in-house criminal expertise by terrorist groups to help meet operational requirements. For terrorist groups, the incentive to develop such capabilities is obvious as proceeds from illicit streams can provide a sizable and reliable source of funding.

## Terrorists Become Organized Crime

Indeed, the attraction of such funding has prompted analysts to suggest that lucrative illicit activities may eventually transform politically motivated groups into bona fide criminal organizations. As terrorists become increasingly involved in commercial enterprises, their interest in making a profit gradually overrides political aspirations. Frequently cited in this regard is the Revolutionary Armed Forces of Colombia (FARC), although the evidence is disputed. In the end, it becomes difficult to judge a group's motivation for engaging in organized crime, especially as motivations can vary among the group's members.

Frustratingly, empirical evidence for the organized crime-terror nexus is notoriously scarce. This, in turn, makes it difficult to determine precisely which aspects of the nexus are the most significant. The handful of examples that are frequently cited suggest that terrorist groups engaging in organized crime for fund-raising purposes represent the strongest link—with the drug trade playing a particularly prominent role. But this pattern is hardly a recent phenomenon. Rebels, guerrillas and insurgent shave long used organized crime and illicit revenue streams to finance their political agendas. Indeed, further historical analysis of the relationship between organized crime and rebel activities—in places like Colombia, Sierra Leone and Kosovo—may provide further useful insights.

Organized crime is also just one form of terrorist financing among many—including donations, legal businesses and common crime—andbrings with it some obvious risks to terrorist groups. Involvement in organized crime can compromise legitimacy and popular support, distract from political goals, and invite the full force of domestic (and on occasion international) law enforcement activities. Moreover, building an effective organized crime-terror nexus requires additional skills and infrastructure.[2] While individual terrorist cells can engage in sporadic crime, organized crime requires more permanent structures, transnational networks and logistics. Whether a terrorist group engages in organized crime is thus not only contingent on the cost of its operations, but also on its operational capabilities.[3]

The potential for cooperation between organized crime and terrorist groups should lead to governments and law enforcement agencies developing assertive and coordinated counter-strategies. Preventing OC and terrorism from working together—or from generating a cumulative impact that further weakens vulnerable states—will be difficult if efforts to fight organized crime and terrorism remain in separate portfolios. Understanding the factors that contribute to the emergence of OC and terrorist groups—not to mention the possibilities of cooperation between them—will not only make states more resilient, but also more effective in ensuring that the crime-terrorism nexus becomes more risky and less profitable. Counter-strategies must not be limited to making police more effective and borders tighter. Improving public services, generating employment in the licit economy and establishing a reliable legal environment can be just as important for the overall resilience of states.

## Notes

1. Louise I. Shelley and John T. Picarelli, "Methods Not Motives: Implications of the Convergence of International Organized Crime and Terrorism," *Police Practice and Research: An International Journal*, vol. 3, no. 4, 2002, pp. 305–318.

2. Michael Freeman, "The Sources of Terrorism Financing: Theory and Typology," *Studies in Conflict and Terrorism*, vol. 34, no. 6, June 1, 2011, pp. 461–475.

3. Steven Hutchinson and Pat O'Malley, "Crime-Terror Nexus?: Thinking on Some of the Links Between Terrorism and Criminality," *Studies in Conflict and Terrorism*, vol. 30, no. 12, December 2007, pp. 1095–1107.

> "The United States should pursue broad charges against those who led America's leading investment banks and other financial institutions to the brink of collapse."

# RICO Should Be Used to Prosecute Wall Street Criminals

## Michael Moran

*Michael Moran argues in the following viewpoint that white-collar Wall Street criminals should be treated like organized crime members and that the RICO (antiracketeering) law should be used to prosecute them for their crimes. He contends that neither the current administration nor previous administrations have been tough enough on white-collar criminals, and this lack of enforcement has resulted in more white-collar crimes being committed. Moran believes that allowing the banking firms to settle in court gives them an easy way to avoid criminal charges and sets the precedent that white-collar crime is acceptable. Moran is a journalist and the author of* The Reckoning: Debt, De-

Michael Moran, "Let's Teach Wall Street—the Land of TARP, MBSs, and SIVs—a New Acronym: RICO," *Slate*, December 13, 2011. Copyright © 2011 by Michael Moran. All rights reserved. Reproduced by permission.

mocracy and the Future of American Power, *as well as an executive at Control Risks, an international political risk and security consulting firm.*

As you read, consider the following questions:

1. What does Moran say that the Obama administration should do about the crimes committed on Wall Street?

2. Moran argues that even if the prosecution of white-collar criminals failed, pursuing such cases would do what?

3. The author points out that RICO laws have been used against whom?

What in God's name is wrong with the SEC? The Securities and Exchange Commission—spoken of as though it has the power to destroy entire economies with a single question—continues to engage in settlement talks with banks caught red-handed defrauding investors and who know that the $285 million or so they'll have to pay to the federal government as a result would barely register on their books.

And yet this persists. Late last month [November 2011], as we were still recovering from our Thanksgiving turkey, U.S. District Court Judge Jed Rakoff threw out another kind of turkey—one presented by the SEC to his court. Citigroup, which like many other banks regularly created "investment vehicles" for clients that it then bet on to fail, had agreed to pay $285 million to prevent these practices from being dragged through the courts, or admitting guilt, which would not only be embarrassing (though at this point, could shame really matter?) but also potentially expose senior executives to criminal charges.

"Criminal Charges." Imagine that. Yes, I know, attorneys regularly cut such deals to save court costs or, perhaps, because they worry the charges might not stick at trial. But let's face it, the American public—right, left and center—has had it with white-collar criminals being treated as "overzealously creative" while teenage shoplifters are threatened with jail. The SEC's response—to petition Congress for the right to raise the fines—is not enough. These cases should not be settled; the settlements send a message of impotence that will come back to haunt us.

## Current Banking Laws Do Not Work

The reforms of banking regulation and securities law in the United States and Europe have been uncoordinated and, while sometimes useful, often blunted and sidestepped by the financial industry. Amazingly, the market for over-the-counter derivatives—the SIVs (structured investment vehicles) and MBSs mortgage-backed securities and CDSs (credit default swaps) that dragged the world towards the abyss in 2008—remains almost entirely unregulated. Thirteen years after Brooksley Born, then-chairwoman of the Commodities Futures Trading Commission, warned in the 1990s that this market concealed a ticking timebomb, and four years since it detonated, trillions of dollars worth of transactions that tie American banks to their counterparties around the world remain opaque.

Born was shutdown by Wall Street's [President Bill] Clinton-era guardians of the day—Alan Greenspan, Robert Rubin and Larry Summers. Similarly, efforts to reimpose the Glass-Steagal separations of commercial and investment banking after the 2008 debacle also failed. This, for now, appears to be the state of play—American democracy, entangled in the political complexities of legislative wrangling, has chosen to cross its fingers rather than put up its dukes.

## Prosecuting Wall Street Criminals

But the Obama administration can still do a great deal of good by simply rediscovering its stomach for prosecution. The Justice Department in the United States should pursue broad charges against those who led America's leading investment

## Federal Court Judges in New York Give White-Collar Criminals Less than Minimum Sentences

| Judge | Average sentence (months) | Number of sentences | Percentage sentencing below minimum guideline |
|---|---|---|---|
| Paul Crotty | 17 months | 3 | 20% |
| Richard Holwell | 60 | 3 | 39% |
| Jed Rakoff | 21 | 6 | 38% |
| Richard Sullivan | 55.7 | 7 | 6% |

Judges with at least three sentences from 2010 to present. Excludes government cooperators.
Source: WJS research, *Wall Street Journal*.

TAKEN FROM: Michael Rothfield, "In Gupta Sentencing, a Judgment Call," *Wall Street Journal*, October 10, 2012.

banks and other financial institutions to the brink of collapse in 2008. Focusing on fraudulent claims about the performance of complex securitized financial products—products sold as AAA risks—should be possible, particularly if the Justice Department employs the RICO (Racketeer Influenced and Corrupt Organizations) statutes that helped bring the U.S. mafia down to size two decades ago.

Astoundingly, when [investment firm] Goldman Sachs was found to have sold subprime mortgage products that it specifically designed to fail—in part so that a major client, Paulson & Company, could bet against it—the government accepted a 2010 settlement offer rather than continue with a criminal case. The settlement was a record $550 million. That's a rounding error on Paulson's balance sheet (though they had a miserable 2010, it must be said, as karma apparently has finally taken a hand).

But pursuing such cases to their legal end, even if the prosecution somehow failed, would restore credibility to U.S.

regulators and ultimately have a much more profound effect on the financial sector. Instead, the government sent a message that, yes, it may pursue charges in egregious cases, but the option to pay it off will remain.

Clearly, RICO was not designed for Wall Street. But then, back in the mid-1980s, the National Organization for Women used RICO to file suit against radical anti-abortion groups that had gone beyond protesting and actually physically blocked women from entering clinics providing abortion services (not to mention those that simply existed in order to blow them up). The case went to the Supreme Court, which ultimately ruled in 1994 that RICO could be applied to a political organization.

It's worth noting that the entire case rested on whether RICO could be applied to an entity, like the anti-abortion movement, which wasn't in business to make a profit. I highly doubt that issue presents much of an obstacle with Wall Street.

# Periodical and Internet Sources Bibliography

*The following articles have been selected to supplement the diverse views presented in this chapter.*

| | |
|---|---|
| Tania Arroyo | "Drug War: Faster and More Furious," *Foreign Policy in Focus*, September 27, 2011. |
| Lawrence Delevinge | "The Unsmokables," *New York*, June 16, 2008. |
| Shachar Eldar | "Holding Organized Crime Leaders Accountable for the Crimes of Their Subordinates," *Criminal Law and Philosophy*, June 2012. |
| Douglas M. Fraser and Renee P. Novakoff | "Getting It Right to Forestall a New National Security Threat," *Joint Force Quarterly*, April 2013. |
| Joshua Hammer | "Defying the Godfather," *Smithsonian*, October 2010. |
| Alex Kinsbury | "War on Gangs," *U.S. News & World Report*, December 15, 2008. |
| Robert M. Lombardo | "Fighting Organized Crime: A History of Law Enforcement Efforts in Chicago," *Journal of Contemporary Criminal Justice*, May 2013. |
| Joseph Wheatley | "The Flexibility of RICO and Its Use on Street Gangs Engaging in Organized Crime in the United States," *Policing: Journal of Policy and Practice*, 2008. |
| Claire Yorke and Benôit Gomis | "Changing the Prescription," *World Today*, August/September 2012. |

OPPOSING
VIEWPOINTS®
SERIES

CHAPTER 4

# Has Organized Crime Moved Online?

# Chapter Preface

The "European Union Serious and Organized Crime Threat Assessment" report issued in 2013 by Europol, a collective law enforcement organization operating across Europe, cited the Internet as the latest venue for emerging criminal activity. While outlaw organizations still run more-traditional illegal commerce such as the drug trade, Europol claims that many of these groups are turning to the virtual world to expand their operations. Paraphrasing the report, a March newsletter published by CSO security systems reiterates that the Internet "enables organized crime groups to access a large pool of victims, obscure their activities and carry out a diverse range of criminal acts in a shorter period of time and on a much larger scale than ever before." John P. Mello Jr., the author of the newsletter, emphasizes that organized crime also favors the global reach of the Internet and the difficulty of tracing crooked dealings across networks that link all parts of the world. The United Nations Interregional Crime and Justice Research Institute asserts that cybercrime is now a billion-dollar industry that, in the hands of organized crime syndicates, includes fraud, extortion, and theft.

One lucrative activity that attracts organized crime is identity theft. A provocative and much-used phrase today, *identity theft* entails the stealing of personal information such as Social Security numbers, driver's license numbers, and credit card numbers for the purpose of committing fraud. In 2004, the US Secret Service concluded a sting operation that nabbed twenty-eight individuals from eight US states and six countries who were part of a ring of identity thieves. According to an October 2004 *Computerworld* article, Operation Firewall agents found 1.7 million credit card numbers among the records of the thieves, and financial institutions contacted in the aftermath estimated that transactions using these hijacked accounts collectively cost $4.3 million in losses. The Bureau of Justice Statistics holds that in the United States alone, 8.6 million households had a member who was a victim of identity theft in 2010, the most recent year reported.

As previously mentioned, identity theft is only one facet of organized crime online. In a March 2012 *Techworld* article, John E. Dunn discusses the findings of the "Organised Crime in the Digital Age" report by BAE Systems Detica, a cybersecurity company. The report maintains that up to 80 percent of cybercrime is committed by organized gangs. Dunn quotes Kenny McKenzie, head of law enforcement for BAE, as saying, "Organised criminal activity has now moved from being an emerging aspect of cybercrime to become a central feature of the digital crime landscape." Fighting this growing threat, however, has proved challenging. In 2011, the White House released its "Strategy to Combat Transnational Organized Crime," a paper outlining proposed policies, meant, in part, to thwart cybercrime. The president's strategy included increasing private sector awareness of transnational crime, preventing or disrupting criminal activity in emerging markets, and instituting an "international capacity to forensically exploit and judicially process digital evidence." Building on past successes—such as Operation Firewall, the White House hopes that giving more tools and information to government protection agencies will lead to more arrests, thus establishing disincentives for criminals to undertake cybercrime.

Whether the president's mandate will curb this illegal but fruitful enterprise is uncertain. Accessing the Internet and therefore global populations is easy, and the anonymity afforded by virtual connections makes the temptation for illicit activity hard to resist. The experts collected in the following chapter offer their views on organized crime's online pursuits, gauging the threat they pose and whether these shady operations can be stopped in an ever-expanding digital world.

> *"Just as the need to fight organized crime led to the RICO statutes, Congress is likely to pass laws to make it easier to fight cybercrime."*

# Hacktivists Must Be Fought Like Organized Criminals

*Hal Berenson*

*Hal Berenson argues in the following viewpoint that cybercriminals, or "hacktivists," progressed in their activities from small, isolated cyberattacks to major crimes and have gotten the attention of the FBI and other US government agencies in doing so. He points to the cyberactivist group known as Anonymous as being dangerous to both national and personal security for Americans. Berenson believes that because this loosely affiliated group has recently gone after federal organizations, they will be soon found and prosecuted in order to protect both the country's government and citizens. Berenson is president of the True Mountain Group, which provides technology and management consulting, after retiring from Microsoft, where he was a general manager and engineer.*

As you read, consider the following questions:

1. Berenson cites FBI director Robert Mueller as saying what about cybercrime in the United States?

2. To what does the author point as evidence of the US Congress's concern about cybercrime?

3. Berenson says that hacktivism should matter even to people who support its political goals because it has become a leading cause of what?

Over the last couple of weeks [early March 2012] we've seen the FBI and international law enforcement groups arrest members of the LulzSec and Anonymous groups for their computer hacking activities. For the last five years or so these (and other) groups had been launching an accelerating set of attacks on commercial and governmental computer systems. Since they weren't doing it for profit, and instead seemed motivated largely by personal political leanings, this was all considered "hacktivism". Of course the activities were criminal. Of course these "super-hackers" used technology to hide themselves from the authorities. And, in truth, as long as their activities were limited to minor stunts meant to send political messages, law enforcement wasn't going to put a lot of resources into stopping them. But they were so righteous (particularly in their attempts to support WikiLeaks), and thought themselves made so invincible by the anonymity they maintained on the web, that they fell victim to two mistakes. They accelerated their activities to the point that they woke the sleeping giant. And they forgot that law enforcement has a long history of dealing with "organized crime". In the end they were knocked down a couple of notches by classic law enforcement techniques. More importantly they woke the FBI up to the increasing risk of cybercrime, to the point that a few days ago FBI Director Robert Mueller told RSA [a security firm] Conference attendees that cybercrime was on its way to eclipsing terrorism as the greatest threat to the United States and that the FBI was organizing to fight cybercrime using what it had learned in the fight against terrorism. Legislation for fighting cybercrime is also now a hot topic in the U.S. Congress, which should have us all both relieved and terrified at the same time (since generally speaking law enforcement has used new powers given to them by Congress to do more than Congress intended, such as apply RICO to non-organized crime activities).

## The LulzSec and Anonymous Story

For those who don't follow the story a very brief summary. A disaffected member of LulzSec (and Anonymous) figures out who a key leader of LulzSec is and this information gets to the FBI. The FBI goes after the leader, and apparently offers to keep him out of prison if he helps bring down the group. The leader cooperates and helps the FBI gather information about group members, their activities, etc. Eventually the FBI decides it has what it needs and the arrests follow. Does this sound much different from how the FBI has brought down organized crime groups in the past? Think "Sammy the Bull" Gravano and the Gambino crime family as a well-known example.

## Cyberattacks Cannot Be Ignored

Think back to the late 1960s and early 1970s where anti-war protests spawned leftist activism groups that used civil disobedience which themselves spawned ever more radical groups that were willing to use violence, like the Weather Underground and its bombings of corporate and government buildings (including the U.S. Capitol). LulzSec and Anonymous were becoming the Weather Underground and Red Army Faction (aka, Baader-Meinhof Gang) of the Internet age. That was something law enforcement couldn't ignore.

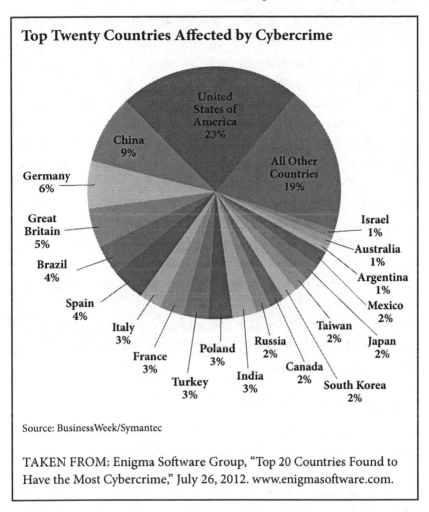

## Top Twenty Countries Affected by Cybercrime

United States of America 23%

All Other Countries 19%

China 9%

Germany 6%

Great Britain 5%

Brazil 4%

Spain 4%

Italy 3%

France 3%

Turkey 3%

Poland 3%

India 3%

Russia 2%

Canada 2%

South Korea 2%

Taiwan 2%

Japan 2%

Mexico 2%

Argentina 1%

Australia 1%

Israel 1%

Source: BusinessWeek/Symantec

TAKEN FROM: Enigma Software Group, "Top 20 Countries Found to Have the Most Cybercrime," July 26, 2012. www.enigmasoftware.com.

Some months ago, when LulzSec launched an attack on the CIA, I tweeted about how silly it was to launch a cyberattack on organizations who've declared that such attacks could warrant a kinetic response. I was only half-joking. Governments, the U.S. included, will use force to stop cyberattacks. Particularly attacks that put lives at risk. In this regard perhaps LulzSec and Anonymous members have been lucky that law enforcement got to them first. If a CIA operative were to lose their life as a result of hacking, I'm not sure the CIA's response would necessarily involve "due process". And if hacking resulted in the CIA, FBI, etc. failing to stop a terrorist attack the public would certainly be calling for blood.

Just as Sammy Gravano's testimony brought down the leadership of the Gambino crime family, but didn't destroy the family, let alone the whole "Cosa Nostra" [Sicilian Mafia], the recent waves of arrests will not eliminate cybercrime, hacktivism, or even the Anonymous group (though it probably did end LulzSec itself). They've just made a temporary dent. But the sleeping giant is awake. Just as the need to fight organized crime led to the RICO statutes, Congress is likely to pass laws to make it easier to fight cybercrime. Just as 9/11 led the FBI and other government agencies to focus on fighting terrorism, they are now organizing and gearing up to fight cybercrime. Likewise, just as 9/11 made companies and government organizations hyperaware of the need for better physical security, the attacks by LulzSec and Anonymous may finally have shaken them up enough to really focus on cybersecurity. And not a moment too soon.

## Waking Up to Cybercrime

In some ways I really want to thank the members of LulzSec and Anonymous for waking up the world to the dangers of cybercrime and hacktivism. A few years back I suffered directly from the result of hacktivism, as a group broke into the web site of a political candidate they didn't like, stole credit card information (including mine), and then released it publicly to embarrass the candidate. Hacktivism has now become a leading cause of identity theft and invasion of privacy, which is why the fight against it should matter to even those who support its political goals. On the other hand I worry about the loss of freedom that might result from fighting hacktivism. For example, during the recent legitimate protest activities against the SOPA [Stop Online Piracy Act] and PIPA [Protect IP (intellectual property) Act] legislation, attempts were made to discredit protesters by suggesting a link with the hacking activities of Anonymous. Will new legislation and zealous law enforcement cross what are often fine lines between legitimate and unacceptable activities? No doubt. And that's something we'll all have to be on guard for.

Have we entered a new era in the fight against cybercrime, and its Hacktivism guise? I think so. The next few years are likely to be exciting and (hopefully just electronically) bloody. Or maybe we'll all get lulled back into a false sense of security until a cyber-9/11 occurs. But with any luck we can combine an active fight against cybercriminals and hacktivists with the continued march towards systems that are significantly harder to hack to relegate this problem to "just" another part of society's darker side. Sadly that is the best we can hope for.

> "Hacktivists have felt the force of the
> United States government ... and all
> reflect an alarming contrast between
> the severity of the punishment and the
> flimsiness of the actual charges."

# Hacktivists as Gadflies

*Peter Ludlow*

*In the viewpoint that follows, Peter Ludlow argues that hacktivists are not criminals but more like social activists who point out problems in society and bring them to the public's attention. He compares the group to Socrates, who was persecuted and punished around 400 B.C. for speaking truth to power. He claims that hacktivists are being punished too harshly for their actions, and in some cases, he thinks they should be rewarded for making the public aware of government and political corruption. Ludlow is a professor of philosophy at Northwestern University.*

As you read, consider the following questions:

1. In what ways are hacktivists different from garden-variety hackers, according to Ludlow?

2. As stated by the author, what exactly did Andrew Auernheimer, a hacktivist that went by the online name "Weev," do?

3. What punishment does the author say that Auernheimer received for his hacktivism?

Around 400 B.C., Socrates was brought to trial on charges of corrupting the youth of Athens and "impiety." Presumably, however, people believed then as we do now, that Socrates' real crime was being too clever and, not insignificantly, a royal pain to those in power or, as Plato put it, a gadfly. Just as a gadfly is an insect that could sting a horse and prod it into action, so too could Socrates sting the state. He challenged the moral values of his contemporaries and refused to go along with unjust demands of tyrants, often obstructing their plans when he could. Socrates thought his service to Athens should have earned him free dinners for life. He was given a cup of [poison] hemlock instead.

We have had gadflies among us ever since, but one contemporary breed in particular has come in for a rough time of late: the "hacktivist." While none have yet been forced to drink hemlock, the state has come down on them with remarkable force. This is in large measure evidence of how poignant, and troubling, their message has been.

## Not Ordinary Hackers

Hacktivists, roughly speaking, are individuals who redeploy and repurpose technology for social causes. In this sense they are different from garden-variety hackers out to enrich only themselves. People like Steve Jobs, Steve Wozniak and Bill Gates began their careers as hackers—they repurposed technology, but without any particular political agenda. In the case of Mr. Jobs and Mr. Wozniak, they built and sold "blue boxes," devices that allowed users to defraud the phone company. Today, of course, these people are establishment heroes, and the

## Anonymous's Online Activism

Anonymous in its larger definition is a social activism group empowered by social media sites like Twitter and Facebook. They represent a new type of activism—leaderless, unorganized, rooted in the Internet—with the ability to mobilize a large number of people quickly around a specific issue. The four top Anonymous-related Twitter accounts (*@anonops, @AnonymousIRC, @Anonymous, @Lulzsec*) have more than 800,000 followers, giving them significant clout. YouTube videos about or from Anonymous get millions of views. During the DDoS attacks on the Justice Department, LOIC [Low Orbit Ion Cannon, an open source software application to test a network's ability to handle stress] saw a large increase in its number of downloads, peaking around 50,000 in a week. Anonymous reported that 5,630 members participated in the attack.

*Sebastien Goasguen, John Hoyt, and Ryan Cooke,*
*"Anonymous: Activist Hackers in the Headlines,"*
Linux Magazine, *January 30, 2012.*

contrast between their almost exalted state and the scorn being heaped upon hacktivists is instructive.

## Some Hacktivists Are Actually Helping

For some reason, it seems that the government considers hackers who are out to line their pockets less of a threat than those who are trying to make a political point. Consider the case of Andrew Auernheimer, better known as "Weev." When Weev discovered in 2010 that AT&T had left private information about its customers vulnerable on the Internet, he and a colleague wrote a script to access it. Technically, he did not "hack" anything; he merely executed a simple version of what Google Web crawlers do every second of every day—sequentially walk through public URLs and extract the content. When he got the information (the e-mail addresses of 114,000 iPad users, including [New York City] Mayor Michael Bloomberg and [Chicago mayor] Rahm Emanuel, then the White House chief of staff), Weev did not try to profit from it; he notified the blog Gawker of the security hole.

For this service Weev might have asked for free dinners for life, but instead he was recently sentenced to 41 months in prison and ordered to pay a fine of more than $73,000 in damages to AT&T to cover the cost of notifying its customers of its own security failure.

When the federal judge Susan Wigenton sentenced Weev on March 18, she described him with prose that could have been lifted from [Socrates'] prosecutor Meletus in Plato's "Apology." "You consider yourself a hero of sorts," she said, and noted that Weev's "special skills" in computer coding called for a more draconian sentence. I was reminded of a line from an essay written in 1986 by a hacker called the Mentor: "My crime is that of outsmarting you, something that you will never forgive me for."

When offered the chance to speak, Weev, like Socrates, did not back down: "I don't come here today to ask for forgiveness. I'm here to tell this court, if it has any foresight at all, that it should be thinking about what it can do to make amends to me for the harm and the violence that has been inflicted upon my life."

He then went on to heap scorn upon the law being used to put him away—the Computer Fraud and Abuse Act, the same law that prosecutors used to go after the 26-year-old Internet activist Aaron Swartz, who committed suicide in January [2013].

The law, as interpreted by the prosecutors, makes it a felony to use a computer system for "unintended" applications, or even violate a terms-of-service agreement. That would theoretically make a felon out of anyone who lied about their age or weight on Match.com.

## Exposing Government Corruption

The case of Weev is not an isolated one. Barrett Brown, a journalist who had achieved some level of notoriety as the "former unofficial not-spokesman for Anonymous," the hacktivist group, now sits in federal custody in Texas. Mr. Brown came under the scrutiny of the authorities when he began poring over documents that had been released in the hack of two private security companies, HBGary Federal and Stratfor. Mr. Brown did not take part in the hacks, but he did become obsessed with the contents that emerged from them—in particular the extracted documents showed that private security contractors were being hired by the United States government to develop strategies for undermining protesters and journalists, including Glenn Greenwald, a columnist for *Salon*. Since the cache was enormous, Mr. Brown thought he might crowdsource the effort and copied and pasted the URL from an Anonymous chat server to a Web site called Project PM, which was under his control.

Just to be clear, what Mr. Brown did was repost the URL from a Web site that was publicly available on the Internet. Because Stratfor had not encrypted the credit card information of its clients, the information in the cache included credit card numbers and validation numbers. Mr. Brown didn't extract the numbers or highlight them; he merely offered a link to the database. For this he was charged on 12 counts, all of which pertained to credit card fraud. The charges against him add up to about 100 years in federal prison. It was "virtually impossible," Mr. Greenwald, wrote recently in [British newspaper] *The Guardian*, his new employer, "to conclude that the obscenely excessive prosecution he now faces is unrelated to that journalism and his related activism."

Other hacktivists have felt the force of the United States government in recent months, and all reflect an alarming contrast between the severity of the punishment and the flimsiness of the actual charges. The case of Aaron Swartz has been well documented. Jeremy Hammond, who reportedly played a direct role in the Stratfor and HBGary hacks, has been in jail for more than a year awaiting trial. Mercedes Haefer, a journalism student at the University of Nevada, Las Vegas, faces charges for hosting an Internet Relay Chat channel where an Anonymous denial of service attack was planned. Most recently, Matthew Keys, a 26-year-old social-media editor at Reuters, who allegedly assisted hackers associated with Anonymous (who reportedly then made a prank change to a *Los Angeles Times* headline), was indicted on federal charges that could result in more than $750,000 in fines and prison time, inciting a new outcry against the law and its overly harsh enforcement. The list goes on.

In a world in which nearly everyone is technically a felon, we rely on the good judgment of prosecutors to decide who should be targets and how hard the law should come down on them. We have thus entered a legal reality not so different from that faced by Socrates when the Thirty Tyrants ruled Athens, and it is a dangerous one. When everyone is guilty of something, those most harshly prosecuted tend to be the ones that are challenging the established order, poking fun at the authorities, speaking truth to power—in other words, the gadflies of our society.

*"[Chinese] cyber-security exploits against American targets are not the only ones. Huge damage is also being done by organised crime."*

# Organized Crime Hackers Threaten American Infrastructure

## The Economist

*In the viewpoint that follows,* The Economist *suggests that too much emphasis is being placed on Chinese hackers, and not enough attention is being paid to organized domestic hackers. The author equates these organized hackers with organized criminals and claims they are gaining access to businesses' secure information, putting everyone at risk and costing billions of dollars a year. Further, the author argues that the Chinese hackers that do commit cyberattacks against the United States are not employed by the Chinese government, but are organized criminals. In order to combat this organized cybercrime, the author urges businesses and individuals to be proactive in their attempts to defend themselves, their privacy, and their money against this new breed of organized crime.* The Economist *is a weekly news publication providing articles and editorials on a range of internationally pertinent topics and issues.*

As you read, consider the following questions:

1. According to the author, Systematic, a security-software provider, estimates that global cybercrime costs businesses approximately how much a year?

2. In the author's view, why are fears of Chinese hackers overstated?

3. What is one reason given by the author for why there is no doubt that cyber crime is increasing?

Chinese hackers may get all the notoriety, but their cyber-security exploits against American targets are not the only ones. Huge damage is also being done by organised crime. This past week [early March 2013], a large metropolitan utility in the United States announced it had suffered a massive "distributed denial of service" (DDoS) attack, knocking out its automated online—and telephone—payment systems and forcing 155,000 customers to pay their bills in person over the ensuing 48 hours.

At its peak, the utility's back-end computers that run its customer database were flooded with 5.7m spurious packets of data a second, bringing all legitimate transactions to a standstill. On the second day of the attack, the utility called in Prolexic Technologies. Based in Florida, Prolexic maintains "scrubbing centres" around America, Europe and Asia to suck up such malevolent deluges. The attack on the utility was identified as originating within the United States.

Make no mistake, the attackers were not pranksters bent on causing mischief. Nor was the attack a simple "smash and grab" aimed at stealing a few passwords. The kind of perpetrators involved were hardened criminals who use rented "botnets" to extort money from their victims, or to steal intellectual property, industrial secrets and marketing plans for sale to rivals at home and abroad.

## Big Business for Organized Criminals

This is big business now organised crime has access to automated exploit-kits and cloud-based software services that are every bit as sophisticated as (some say even more so than) those used by Fortune 500 companies. No longer do criminals need their own tame programmers. They can rent all the crimeware services they need to infiltrate a target's computer network invisibly, and remain undetected for months or years while siphoning off secrets for sale.

How many firms pay the ransom or buy the phony "remedial solutions" to get their businesses back up and running is anyone's guess. Various figures circulate for the cost of doing business with cyber-criminals. Symantec, a large security-software provider famous for its Norton Antivirus products, estimates that global cyber-crime costs victims $110 billion a year in remediation and lost business as well as ransom payments.

That is probably a reasonable guess (other security-software firms put the figure far higher). Shawn Henry, a former assistant director of the Federal Bureau of Investigation, told Congress recently about how one company had all its data on a ten-year, $1 billion research programme copied by hackers in a single night.

## Fears of Chinese Hackers Are Overstated

While it may make headlines, fears that attacks by the People's Liberation Army and other Chinese hackers could wreak havoc on America's critical infrastructure—especially, its oil and gas pipelines, electricity and water supplies, wireless networks, air-traffic control systems, even its missile defences—are overblown. The Chinese have far too much at stake to risk such provocation.

What China's cyber-crooks are focused on plain and simple is theft. They are out to steal all the industrial secrets they can from America's high-tech firms—especially those with advanced "fracking" technology for extracting natural gas and tight oil from shales and rocks deep underground. By all accounts, the authorities in Beijing are concerned that an energy-independent America could shift the global balance of power in a significant way.

In a sense, though, the victims of such attacks have only themselves to blame. Many organisations have a false sense of security, complacency even, as a result of having invested heavily in security tools in the past. Yet "non-agile" defences like passwords, firewalls and antivirus software, as well as intrusion-detection and prevention systems have become less than effective now attackers have started using encryption and other tricks to evade them, notes Deloitte & Touche, a management consultancy.

Most websites keep usernames and passwords in master files that are "hashed" with software which encrypts both the username and the password together, so no one can see the plain-text version of either. When someone attempts to log in, the website automatically encrypts both the username and password entered. It then determines whether the hash matches the one stored in the site's user database. If not, a well-designed site will freeze the account after a limited number of unsuccessful attempts to gain access.

## "Spear-Phishing"

That is why most cyber-criminals go "spear-phishing" instead. This involves targeting a low-level individual in an organisation using an e-mail scam that fools the hapless individual into visiting a tainted website. Once there, a malicious tag (called an "iframe") in the HTML code responsible for the page's appearance is injected into the visitor's browser. The inserted malware can be a virus, a Trojan or, most likely, a keylogger. This watches for the user's log on and password, and reports the keystrokes back to the attackers. It is then only a short step to stealing secrets from the victim's employer.

## Cyberattacks Could Leave Millions of Americans Without Power

"The modern thief can steal more with a computer than with a gun. Tomorrow's terrorist may be able to do more damage with a keyboard than with a bomb." These sentences are from the first paragraph of a 1991 National Research Council report, *Computers at Risk*. In the summer of 2010, the emergence of the Stuxnet worm demonstrated that these words were not hyperbole. Unlike most previous cyber intrusions, which exfiltrate computerized information, Stuxnet caused physical damage to centrifuges at the Iranian uranium enrichment plant at Natanz—damage that could just as well have been caused by a bomb. Although it came as no surprise to any serious cybersecurity analyst that genuine attacks—attacks with physical effects—could be made via computer, Stuxnet was a very loud wake-up call to policy makers, political analysts, and the general public around the world. For many observers, Stuxnet raises the possibility that a cyberattack on the US electrical power grid or other critical infrastructure might be catastrophic, and the prospect that large regions of the United States might be without electricity, for example, for many months is frightening, to say the least.

*Herbert Lin, "A Virtual Necessity:*
*Some Modest Steps Toward Greater Cybersecurity"*
Bulletin of the Atomic Scientists, *May 2012.*

Having gained access to the target network, attackers usually run the standard application for accessing databases known as SQL (Structured Query Language). A query is sent to the database masquerading as an innocent request for information, but is really a malicious command designed to reveal confidential data, such as credit-card names and numbers. Literally millions of databases that reside behind websites have been compromised by SQL-injection.

But that is only the half of it. Over the past five years, web attackers have combined forces with botnet operators, who rent their armies of zombie computers to shady organisations responsible for spam, fraud and other nefarious activities. As Mary Landesman, a noted cyber-crime writer, has observed, organised crime has embraced the cloud with a vengeance, and begun delivering "malware as a service" through these powerful distributed networks of infected computers.

Meanwhile, two particularly nasty pieces of crimeware have emerged from the hacking underworld. One is an exploit kit known as Blackhole, which invisibly redirects someone visiting a legitimate website to a compromised site where malware can be loaded. Meanwhile, the victim never knows his browser has left the legitimate site. Cyber-criminals can rent access to Blackhole software by the day or lease a Blackhole server for periods of three months to a year at a time. Today, it accounts for about a third of all detected threats, says Sophos, a data-security firm based in Britain.

The other piece of crimeware to be aware of is a rootkit called ZeroAccess. Like all rootkits, ZeroAccess is capable of hiding its presence from all normal methods of detection, while maintaining privileged access to a computer's inner workings. Because it is effectively invisible to security software, cyber-criminals use it for secretly installing other malware, including Blackhole. With its invisibility cloak, ZeroAccess lets attackers exploit a compromised network for months or even years on end.

There is no doubt that cyber-crime is on the increase. One reason is simply that the Internet was conceived without any form of security in mind. Another is that social media like Facebook and Twitter have made it insanely easy to gather information about a person or a business—and thereby build persuasive scams that exploit human weaknesses to penetrate a network's outer perimeter.

## Making People Aware of the Threat

What is to be done? In a recent blog, Tyler Durden of Kaspersky Lab, a computer-security company with headquarters in Moscow and branches around the world, says that essentially it is a matter of impressing people, at a personal level, about the seriousness of the threat. "It's not about IPs, firewalls, ports and protocols any more. . . . Building secure perimeters and adding corporate policies and certificates is great, but [such things] are starting to become useless."

The trouble is people use their own devices—smartphones, tablets and laptops—for corporate as well as private tasks. They also use their social-media accounts and cloud services like Dropbox to send and receive important data. As far as company policies are concerned, the computer-security situation is out of control. Today is a paradise for attackers, says Mr Durden.

The good news is that the threat of cyber-crime is being seen increasingly as a business opportunity. There are more venture start-ups in data security today than at any time in recent decades. Meanwhile, governments have begun to take the problem seriously.

As Mr Durden notes, everyone at the recent RSA 2013 [security conference], the computer-security world's annual shindig, was talking about Barack Obama's executive order—"in a good way". In his state-of-the-union address last month [February 2013], the president decreed that America's cyber-defences should be strengthened by the increasing of information sharing, and the development of standards to protect the country's national security, its jobs and its people's privacy. The security industry waits to learn how these fine words translate into action. So, presumably, do the cyber-criminals.

I "The image of a highly organised cyber-
underworld run by hardcore criminals
is not the order of the day."

# Most Cybercrime
# Is Not Committed by
# Organized Criminals

*Brian Prince*

*In the viewpoint that follows, Brian Prince argues that most cy-
bercrime in Russia is, contrary to popular belief, committed by
regular hackers, not organized criminals. Prince cites a study
that suggests organized criminals in Russia stay away from petty
cybercrime for the most part. He asserts that this is because there
is too much to lose and not enough to gain from such crime.
Prince concludes that most cybercrimes are perpetrated by computer geeks trying to make a quick and easy buck. Prince is a
journalist who contributes to a number of cybersecurity-focused
publications.*

As you read, consider the following questions:

1. According to the author, who are most of the cyber-
   criminals in Russia?

2. Why, in Prince's view, is there no need for cybercriminals to be part of a classic Mafia?

3. According to the findings of the study cited by the author, if there is any mob involvement in cybercrime what is it mostly doing?

When people think of cyber-crime, the typical image being pushed today is that of highly organised criminal operations. New research, however, suggests the underbelly of cyberspace may be less Mafia-like than some think.

The exploits of Russian cyber-criminals are widely reported. For instance, a checque scam was exposed at last month's [July 2010] Black Hat event, and last year [2009], it was alleged at the RSA [a cybersecurity firm] show in London, that network provider the Russian Businesss Network, was aided by both Internet registrars and the Russian police.

In an effort to improve the level of understanding of today's black hats [cybercriminals], security researchers Fyodor Yarochkin and "The Grugq" have spent several months looking at Russian hacker forums.

"It is an ongoing project that we started about 18 months ago," Grugq told eWEEK. "Originally it started when Fyodor investigated some service offerings from Russian hacker forums for a specific project that I was working on. It turned out to be extremely interesting and amusing, so we discussed doing more long-term monitoring on the forums. It grew from there into what is now a continuous monitoring program." Their research was presented last month at the Hack in the Box 2010 conference in Amsterdam.

## "Geeks, Not Gangsters"

What the two found was that the image of a highly organised cyber-underworld run by hardcore criminals is not the order of the day. Instead, the dozen or so hacker forums they analysed illustrated that many of the users are "geeks, not gangsters," the researchers said.

"Basically, from what we've seen on the forums much of what goes on with the sales of services is much more petty criminal activity, or crimes of opportunity," Grugq said. "Often poor students who like to hack for fun will sell access to a server they've owned. Many don't even realise that this is an illegal activity. This sale will be for $20 or $30 (£13 or £19), which is a lot of money for a poor student in Russia, but for a hardened criminal mastermind bent on destroying Western civilization—not so much."

Similarly, many of the sales of stolen assets tend to be at a very low price point, Yarochkin said. Even a distributed denial of service attack only costs $80 (£51.50) a day to carry out, he added.

"These are not prices that are attractive to serious criminals," he said.

"In terms of percentage, there'd be two to three guys working on stuff professionally, versus 10 to 20 hobbyists," he continued. "Most of the activity is essentially petty criminal activity where guys are trying to make a little extra cash on the side. You can think of it as a self-organising hierarchical system with needs and people able to provide goods and services to satisfy the needs."

Other security pros agreed with the researchers' general characterisation. Though there are "top-feeders" that set up affiliate programs to maximise their profit and let lower-level criminals do the dirty work, these are the closest examples of "mob bosses" to be found, said Joe Stewart, director of malware research at SecureWorks' Counter Threat Unit.

Most participants are students with computer skills that have "grown up with this underground economy and have found a niche for themselves in the criminal marketplace," he said.

"Given the ease of anonymous money transfer in Russia, there's no need for criminals to be part of a classic Mafia gang where they work for a boss, everyone meets in person and

## The Media Have Exaggerated the Cybercrime Threat

In September 2007, the cyber-security group Symantec published their seventh *Internet Security Threat Report*. It found that in "the first half of 2007, 212,101 new malicious code threats were reported to Symantec. This is a 185 percent increase over the second half of 2006". In the week following its publication, the report's findings became the basis for many news stories that were published in reliable and less reliable news print and broadcast outlets. The news story bylines continued a long-standing line of reporting that portrays cybercrime as immensely prevalent and threatening. It is a practice that inevitably shapes and raises public and also media expectations of its impacts. These expectations contrast dramatically with the actual experience of cybercrime within the criminal justice system.

David S. Wall,
"Cybercrime, Media and Insecurity:
The Shaping of Public Perceptions of Cybercrime,"
International Review of Law, Computers,
and Technology, *March–July 2008.*

there is some sort of trust/fear relationship that protects the organisation and its leaders," Stewart said. "What you have these days is organised but they don't necessarily know each other's real name or ever meet in person, and trust is earned by reputation in past transactions."

The level of discourse on the forums is typically similar to 4chan or other online communities where users bicker and snipe at each other, Grugq said. Users who are respected are blessed with endorsements; those who aren't can be blacklisted, he said.

Just about everything is for sale: Skype accounts, botnet software, domain names and dedicated servers, and much, much more.

"Credit cards [are] getting more attention from authorities," Yarochkin said. "So for credit card trading, there are mostly specific, closed forums where you'd need to buy your access. Everything else is being traded in the open."

## The Mob Is Not the Organizer

Yarochkin noted that there are criminal groups operating outside the forums the two analysed that would therefore be invisible to the duo.

"From what we can guess," Grugq said, "any [mob] involvement is more along the lines of some people at the very top of the stack have to pay off the real gangsters. . . . So, for example, if you are organising a massive credit card cash-out scam which nets millions of dollars, you'll have to pay protection money to the mob to not get robbed. It doesn't look like the mob itself is organising these cash-outs though.

"We're not disputing that organised crime is involved with cyber-crime, but the popular conception of leather jacketed thugs running around with firearms and laptops is not in line with what we have observed from the actual communities," he said. "It seems like it is very useful for some companies to popularise the scary idea of Russian cyber-gangsters, but honestly the involvement seems to be much more hands off."

# Periodical and Internet Sources Bibliography

*The following articles have been selected to supplement the diverse views presented in this chapter.*

| | |
|---|---|
| Max Alexander | "Cyber Thieves!," *Reader's Digest*, August 2010. |
| *The Economist* | "An Anonymous Foe," June 18, 2011. |
| Greg Farrell, Michael Riley, and Barrett Sheridan | "From Want Ads to Wanted Posters," *Bloomberg Businessweek*, August 8, 2011. |
| Erika Fry | "Who are the Hackers?," *Fortune*, February 25, 2013. |
| Paul Hyman | "Cybercrime: It's Serious, but Exactly How Serious?," *Communications of the ACM*, March 2013. |
| Erik Larkin | "Organized Crime Moves Into Data Theft," *PC World*, July 2009. |
| Jonathan Lusthaus | "How Organised Is Organised Cybercrime?," *Global Crime*, February 2013. |
| Matthew O'Deane | "Combatting Gangsters Online," *FBI Law Enforcement Bulletin*, April 2011. |
| John Seabrook | "Network Insecurity," *New Yorker*, May 20, 2013. |
| Jessica Silver-Greenberg | "A Field Day for Cyber-fiends," *Bloomberg Businessweek*, February 9, 2009. |

# For Further Discussion

## Chapter 1

1. Walter Kemp argues that organized crime threatens international security in a variety of ways—pointing out that organized criminals work both against the government and from within. Moisés Naím contends that the biggest threat from organized crime today stems from government officials who have become leaders of organized crime. After reading the two viewpoints, whose view do you find more convincing? Are organized criminals infiltrating governments, or are government officials turning into organized criminals? Is there a difference between the two? Use quotes from the viewpoints to support your answer.

2. Lawrence Harmon maintains that gang activity and violence have pushed communities to a breaking point and made it unsafe (in some cases deadly) for children to go out in their neighborhoods alone. Caspar Walsh, on the other hand, asserts that gangs provide youth with a sense of community and meaningful relationships. In light of the evidence presented by both authors, do you believe that the benefits of gang culture highlighted by Walsh outweigh the negative impacts highlighted by Harmon? Is there a difference between types of gangs, and are the two authors describing the same types of groups? Explain, using specific examples from the viewpoints when making your case.

3. Joy Olson contends that organized crime is at its core a violation of human rights and that the human rights community must take action to combat this international threat. Reporters Without Borders highlights the threat organized crime presents to journalists around the world,

and maintains that without open reporting about the problem, meaningful action will not be taken. Consider the arguments of both authors, and determine which group you believe to be more important to the fight against organized crime—the human rights community or news reporters. Cite the viewpoints to support your claims.

## Chapter 2

1. After reading the viewpoints by the UNODC and Joe Karaganis, how serious do you believe the crime of counterfeiting goods and piracy to be, and does organized crime control these criminal enterprises? Do you agree with the statistics provided by the UNODC that show counterfeit products to be a serious money-making business for organized criminals and a risk to people's health, or do you trust Joe Karaganis's argument that organized crime has little to do with piracy? Support your answer with quotes from the viewpoints.

2. Marc Goodman argues that organized crime has recently adopted many of the tactics used by legitimate business to increase its profits and operate effectively, maintaining that many business leaders could learn from organized crime. Paul Wallis, however, argues that supposedly legitimate businesses on Wall Street have already begun engaging in organized crime activities. Do you think that the authors have taken their arguments too far? Could businesses really learn from organized crime, and is Wall Street really engaging in criminal activity? Why or why not?

## Chapter 3

1. Gary Johnson and Vanda Felbab-Brown both explore the effect of legalizing drugs on cartels. Johnson contends that legalization of marijuana would put a dent in cartels' in-

come and make it difficult for them to operate, but Felbab-Brown asserts that legalization will not have any impact on the cartels' ability to carry on business as usual. Conduct some outside research on the previous effects of legalization or prohibition on criminal activity. Using what you find in combination with the views from these authors, take a stance on the benefits or consequences of legalizing drugs with regard to its impact on organized crime.

2. Gun violence is often a major concern linked with organized crime and gangs. Tiffany Willis maintains that increased gun control would be the most effective way to stop gang violence whereas Michael Geer argues that a ban on guns would only increase gun violence. Both authors provide concrete examples and statistics to support their views. Which author offers better examples or statistics, your opinion? Do you find any flaws with the statistics or examples used by either of the authors? Use specific examples to show whether the authors' use is effective or not.

3. Wibke Hansen focuses on the international cooperation necessary to combat organized crime and terrorism on a global level. Michael Moran focuses on the national laws that should be invoked to prosecute the organized crime he sees businesses committing on Wall Street. Do you believe one of these types of crime presents a larger threat to national and international interests? Should one of these types of organized crime receive greater focus, or should both be addressed equally? Explain.

# Chapter 4

1. Hal Berenson maintains that hacktivists should be treated as criminals, and Peter Ludlow asserts that hacktivists have been wrongly labeled and prosecuted as criminals. With which view do you agree? Are all hacktivists the same, or

should some not be treated as criminals? Use quotes from the viewpoints to support your claims.

2. *The Economist* asserts that organized criminal hacking presents a serious risk to American infrastructure, but Brian Prince assures readers that organized crime syndicates are not the ones who are committing sophisticated cyber-crimes. Why is it important to determine both the people responsible for cybercrime and their targets? Do you think that both viewpoints have accurately portrayed these actors and victims, or have they overlooked important players? Use quotes from the viewpoints to support your claims, pulling in additional outside resources as needed.

# Organizations to Contact

*The editors have compiled the following list of organizations concerned with the issues debated in this book. The descriptions are derived from materials provided by the organizations. All have publications or information available for interested readers. The list was compiled on the date of publication of the present volume; the information provided here may change. Be aware that many organizations take several weeks or longer to respond to inquiries, so allow us much time as possible.*

**Brookings Institution**
1775 Massachusetts Ave. NW, Washington, DC   20036
(202) 797-6000
e-mail: communications@brookings.edu
website: www.brookings.edu

The Brookings Institution is a private nonprofit organization that conducts research with the aim of developing new and effective public policy solutions that make the American democracy stronger, improve the lives of all Americans, and foster an international system that is open, safe, prosperous, and cooperative. As part of its focus on law and justice, Brookings researches corruption, counternarcotics policy, and crime (including organized crime). Articles on these topics, such as "The Impact of Organized Crime on Governance: A Case Study of Nepal" and "Focused Deterrence, Selective Targeting, Drug Trafficking and Organized Crime: Concepts and Practicalities" can be read on the Brookings website.

**CERT Program**
4500 Fifth Ave., Pittsburgh, PA   15213-2612
(412) 268-7090 • fax: (412) 268-6989
e-mail: cert@cert.org
website: www.ccrt.org

The CERT Program was founded in 1988 to provide a concerted response to cybersecurity threats and is located within the Software Engineering Institute at Carnegie Mellon University. Through its collection of scientific data through research and real-world experience, the organization seeks to mitigate Internet security threats and help create more-secure software and Internet access. Details about CERT's work in secure systems, organizational security, coordinated response, and training can all be found on the organization's website.

## Council on Foreign Relations (CFR)

Harold Pratt House, 58 E. 68th St., New York, NY   10065
(212) 434-9400 • fax: (212) 434-9800
website: www.cfr.org

CFR is a nonpartisan public policy think tank that works to provide informative publications to members, policy makers, and the public at large that help advance understanding of all countries' foreign policy options. The council does not take any official position on the issues that it covers. With regard to organized crime around the world, CFR has held symposia to address organized crime and has published transcripts on its website. In addition, the website publishes primary-source documents laying out different organizations' plans for addressing organized crime.

## Federal Bureau of Investigation (FBI)

935 Pennsylvania Ave. NW, Washington, DC   20535-0001
(202) 324-3000
website: www.fbi.gov

The FBI is a national security and law enforcement agency charged with protecting the United States against security threats from international and domestic sources. While much of the organization's work after the September 11, 2001, terrorist attacks has focused on combating terrorism, it remains engaged in fighting crimes such as espionage, cyberattacks, fraud, gangs, and more. The FBI website provides detailed information about modern organized crime and the threat that it presents today, a list of the most wanted criminals, and intelligence reports. Overviews of regional crime threats and programs around the world are available on the FBI website as well.

## Federation of American Scientists (FAS)

1725 DeSales St. NW, 6th Fl., Washington, DC   20036
(202) 546-3300 • fax: (202) 675-1010
e-mail: fas@fas.org
website: www.fas.org

FAS is a national organization that seeks to find policy solutions that will help mitigate national and international security threats through scientific research and analysis. The organization works mainly to stop the legal and illegal proliferation of nuclear weapons and to establish strict standards to ensure nuclear security. FAS has conducted extensive research on the ties between organized crime and nuclear weapons and corruption and published its findings in publications such as "Russian Organized Crime" and "Nations Hospitable to Crime and Terrorism," which are available on its website.

## InSight Crime

Edificio Meridian, Calle 5A, #43B-25, Office 803
Medellín, Antioquia
   Colombia
e-mail: info@insightcrime.org
website: www.insightcrime.org

InSight Crime is a South American organization seeking to advance the research, analysis, and investigation of organized crime in Latin America and the Caribbean in an effort to spur governments to act in the fight against it. News is organized by country on the organization's website, with investigations into specific crimes, gangs, and action being taken on the governmental level to halt criminal activity, including "El Salvador's Gang Truce: Positives and Negatives" and "Country-by-Country Map of Drug Policy Positions in the Americas."

## Interpol

General Secretariat, 200 quai Charles de Gaulle, Lyon   69006
   France
fax: +33 (0)4 72 44 71 63
website: www.interpol.int

Interpol is a neutral international police organization whose membership comes from 190 countries around the world. The group works to coordinate police efforts to improve safety worldwide by providing modern tools, training, expert support, and secure means of communication. The Interpol webpage on organized crime, part of the organization's website, provides a definition of organized crime and details about specific types of criminal networks. Current news and media releases about ongoing organized crime investigations can also be found on this site.

### National Institute of Justice (NIJ)

810 7th St. NW, Washington, DC   20531
(202) 307-2942
website: www.nij.gov

The NIJ is the government agency within the US Department of Justice charged with research, development, and evaluation aimed at advancing the evidence-based understanding of issues related to crime and justice. The organization has researched a range of issues from national and transnational organized crime itself to related topics such as gangs and human trafficking, with publications and additional resources available on the NIJ website.

### Organized Crime and Gang Section of the US Department of Justice (OCGS)

US Department of Justice, Criminal Division, OCGS
1301 New York Ave. NW, Washington, DC   20005
(202) 514-3594
website: www.justice.gov/criminal/ocgs

The OCGS is an office within the US Department of Justice dedicated to combating organized and gang crime by developing and implementing directed approaches to fighting regional, national, and international threats. Transnational organized crime is the main threat addressed by the office. Overviews of these threats can be found on the OCGS website along with access to reports such as "Strategy to Combat Transnational Organized Crime" and "Overview of the Law Enforcement Strategy to Combat International Organized Crime."

## Stockholm International Peace Research Institute North America (SIPRI)

1111 19th St. NW, 12th Fl., Washington, DC   20036
(202) 552-5400 • fax: (202) 238-9604
e-mail: sipri-na@sipri.org
website: www.sipri.org/northamerica

SIPRI North America is the Washington, DC–based SIPRI research center, established in February 2012 to increase cooperation between the Swedish-based institute and North America and to incorporate global perspectives into the institute's work. SIPRI has worked internationally to advance the understanding of the impact of transnational organized crime on global security and to develop programs to fight this threat. Chapters from the organization's annual yearbook, such as chapter 2: "Armed Conflict, Crime and Criminal Violence" from the 2010 edition and focused reports such as "Transnational Organized Crime and Public Health in West Africa" can be found on the SIPRI website.

## United Nations Office on Drugs and Crime (UNODC)

Vienna International Centre, PO Box 500, Vienna   A 1400
  Austria
+43 (1) 26060 • fax: +43 (1) 263-3389
e-mail: info@unodc.org
website: www.unodc.org

The UNODC is the office within the United Nations committed to fighting the spread of illicit drugs and international and organized crime. Since 1997, this organization has worked in cooperation with member states to combat these threats, researched the issues to establish evidence-based grounds for policy making, and assisted states in passing and implementing international treaties that aid local law enforcement in combating organized crime and its related problems. Detailed information about organized crime topics such as corruption, drug trafficking, firearms, and piracy, among others, can be found on the UNODC website. Visitors to the site can also find reports on drugs and human trafficking, statistics about organized crime, and access to the journals *Bulletin on Narcotics* and *Forum on Crime and Society*.

## World Economic Forum USA

3 E. 54th St., 18th Fl., New York, NY   10022
(212) 703-2300 • fax: (212) 703-2399
e-mail: forumusa@weforum.org
website: www.weforum.org

The World Economic Forum USA, the North American affiliate of the World Economic Forum, seeks to make the world a better place by partnering with industry leaders to drive global, regional, and industry agendas. The issues addressed by the organization, at the national and international levels, fall into five main headings: economic growth, environmental sustainability, financial systems, health for all, and social development. The Global Agenda Council on Organized Crime 2012–2013 tackled the issue of organized crime and provided an overview, council insights, further resources, and additional information available through the World Economic Forum website. The report "Organized Crime Enablers" and additional publications can be found on the forum's website as well.

# Bibliography of Books

Jay S. Albanese      *Organized Crime in Our Times.* 6th
                     ed. Burlington, MA: Anderson, 2011.

Jay S. Albanese      *Transnational Crime and the 21st
                     Century: Criminal Enterprise,
                     Corruption, and Opportunity.* New
                     York: Oxford University Press, 2011.

Jack M. Balkin,      *Cybercrime: Digital Cops in a
et al., eds.         Networked Environment.* New York:
                     New York University Press, 2007.

Alan A. Block and    *All Is Clouded by Desire: Global
Constance A.         Banking, Money Laundering, and
Weaver               International Organized Crime.*
                     Westport, CT: Praeger, 2004.

Susan W. Brenner     *Cybercrime: Criminal Threats from
                     Cyberspace.* Santa Barbara, CA:
                     ABC-CLIO, 2010.

Ted Galen            *The Fire Next Door: Mexico's Drug
Carpenter            Violence and the Danger to America.*
                     Washington, DC: Cato Institute,
                     2012.

Misha Glenny         *DarkMarket: How Hackers Became the
                     New Mafia.* New York: Vintage, 2012.

Misha Glenny         *McMafia: A Journey Through the
                     Global Criminal Underworld.* New
                     York: Vintage, 2009.

John M.              *A World of Gangs: Armed Young Men
Hagedorn             and Gangsta Culture.* Minneapolis:
                     University of Minnesota Press, 2008.

Jennifer L. Hesterman — *The Terrorist-Criminal Nexus: An Alliance of International Drug Cartels, Organized Crime, and Terror Groups.* Boca Raton, FL: CRC, 2013.

Peter Lilley — *Dirty Dealing: The Untold Truth About Global Money Laundering, International Crime and Terrorism.* 3rd ed. Philadelphia: Kogan Page, 2006.

Robert M. Lombardo — *Organized Crime in Chicago: Beyond the Mafia.* Urbana: University of Illinois Press, 2013.

Moisés Naím — *Illicit: How Smugglers, Traffickers, and Copycats Are Hijacking the Global Economy.* New York: Anchor, 2006.

R.T. Naylor — *Wages of Crime: Black Markets, Illegal Finance, and the Underworld Economy.* Ithaca, NY: Cornell University Press, 2004.

Carolyn Nordstrom — *Global Outlaws: Crime, Money, and Power in the Contemporary World.* Berkeley: University of California Press, 2007.

Selwyn Raab — *Five Families: The Rise, Decline, and Resurgence of America's Most Powerful Mafia Empires.* New York: Thomas Dunne, 2006.

Mitchel P. Roth — *Organized Crime.* New York: Prentice-Hall, 2009.

Louise Shelley — *Human Trafficking: A Global Perspective.* New York: Cambridge University Press, 2010.

Greg B. Smith — *Nothing but Money: How the Mob Infiltrated Wall Street.* New York: Berkley, 2009.

Kimberley L. Thachuk, ed. — *Transnational Threats: Smuggling and Trafficking in Arms, Drugs, and Human Life.* Westport, CT: Praeger, 2007.

Federico Varese — *Mafias on the Move: How Organized Crime Conquers New Territories.* Princeton, NJ: Princeton University Press, 2011.

David S. Wall — *Cybercrime: The Transformation of Crime in the Information Age.* Malden, MA: Polity, 2007.

# Index

US National Security Council, 16–17
US Secret Service, 138
US Senate Caucus on International Narcotics Control, 68
US State Department, 16

# V

Venezuela, 30, 61–62
Verville, Elizabeth, 16
Vice Lords (gang), 114
Victims of organized crime, 55–56
Vigil, James Diego, 43

# W

Wall, David S., 162
Wall Street
  analogy of, 93–94
  banking laws, 133
  bond raising by cities, 91–93
  buying politicians, 95
  definition of crime and, 94
  overview, 91
  RICO to prosecute criminals, 131–135
  similarities to organized crime, 90–96
  white-collar crime on, 94, 96, 133, 134t
*Wall Street Journal* (newspaper), 69, 100
Wallis, Paul, 90–96

WalMart bribes, 94
Walsh, Caspar, 45–48
War on drugs, 69, 110, 122
*Washington Post* (newspaper), 103
Weev. *See* Auernheimer, Andrew
Wells Fargo Bank, 92
West Africa, 24, 26, 74
Western Union scams, 85
White House Office of National Drug Control Policy, 103
White-collar crime, 94, 96, 133, 134t
Wigenton, Susan, 149
WikiLeaks, 34, 35, 141
Willis, Tiffany, 113–117
Winkler, Theodor H., 25
World Economic Forum, 21
World Health Organization, 73
Wozniak, Steve, 147
WTVF (Nashville TV station), 115

# Y

Yakuza, 88, 108
Yarochkin, Fyodor, 160–163
Youth Advocate Program International, 15

# Z

Zedillo, Ernesto, 69
ZeroAccess, 157
Los Zetas (gang), 50, 52, 59, 60